AUTISM IS THE
FUTURE

The Evolution of
a Different Type of Intelligence

Marlo Payne Thurman, PhD

AUTISM IS THE FUTURE:
The Evolution of a Different Type of Intelligence

All marketing and publishing rights guaranteed to and reserved by:

FUTURE HORIZONS INC.

721 W. Abram Street
Arlington, TX 76013
(800) 489-0727
(817) 277-0727
(817) 277-2270 (fax)
E-mail: info@fhautism.com
www.fhautism.com

ISBN: 9781941765890

Dedication

In gratitude, I dedicate this work to all of the individuals, diagnosed or not, who have shared with me a different way to see, experience, and understand the world. I also thank the countless parents, teachers, therapists, and friends of those with an autism spectrum disorder who, like me, have learned to never give up on those on the spectrum of autism—because finding brilliance, in some form or other, is just around the corner.

I would like to thank all the clients and research participants who made this work possible. I hope I honored your words. Mark Jarrett Carroll, thank you for hours upon hours of reading, editing, and discussing this book. Richard Baxter, I truly appreciate you for nudging Future Horizons to read my work. Jennifer Grace, without you, I would not have been able to put all these ideas together. Last, to all the amazing people at Future Horizons, thanks for your patience in seeing this through.

CONTENTS

INTRODUCTION

My Journey into Neurodiversity

Neurodiversity may be every bit as crucial for the human race as biodiversity is for life in general. Who can say what form of wiring will prove best at any given moment? Cybernetics and computer culture, for example, may favor a somewhat autistic cast of mind. (Harvey Blume, September 1, 1998, Atlantic Magazine*)*

My understanding of neurodiversity began in a large warehouse store where I was crushed by a stack of eighteen twelve-foot-long conference tables and sustained a traumatic brain injury. It was a gusty day in May and, according to court records, the wind caught the edge of a pallet stacked on its end and the contents fell "accordion style," battering my brain and damaging my sensory-motor cortex.

After the accident, my mother told me it was like I died and another person inhabited my body; for a long time, I was that different. After the initial fog of my injury faded (which took about five months) I felt, at the age of thirty, that I had lost most of the qualities I used to define myself—favorite colors, foods, clothing preferences, personality, all these had changed. Furthermore, my sensory system was so different, confused, and over-stimulated that I could not function. I no longer accurately read social cues and body language, frequently drawing criticism for sharing inappropriate details or telling inappropriate jokes. I spoke out of turn and at the wrong time or in the wrong place. My organization and executive functioning skills fell apart as I lost my rote verbal memory and sequencing abilities. I also stopped being able to read books, spell basic words, do simple arithmetic in my head, and I couldn't drive a car without becoming lost or disoriented. Within the year, I also started having seizures.

As bad as the injury was, during the weeks and months that followed I began dreaming in three-dimensional pictures. This happened for the first time a week to the day after my accident. It was as if I could see visual-spatial systems that were in perpetual motion. Prior to my injury, I was trained and had been working as a private practice school psychologist with emphasis in neuropsychological assessment. With my formal training and an ability to internally sense the changes that were happening in my own brain, I also began to "see" certain things more clearly.

I could more fully understand the inner workings and relationships of my own cognition, and because I was still limping along in my practice where I specialized in working with quirky, gifted, and twice-exceptional students, I started watching and learning from my clients. In time, this allowed me to transfer and test new theories and insights in my work. As I did this, I realized that my brain had never worked this way before; although for those I worked with and now more fully understood, theirs did. However, they lacked the language skills that I retained to explain it. Before my injury, my strengths were in language and verbal sequencing, and although I saw pictures in my mind, these were almost always flat and unmoving. Years later, I still can't put most of my 3-D pictures into words, but I finally have come to understand how these images affected and forever changed my overall thinking and innate cognitive processing.

It has now been two decades since my accident and although I never returned to my "old self," I get by as long as I stay rested. I have even learned to function fairly well. Some skills came back, while others never did. I still have extremely poor rote memory. I was able to keep working and, through the years, completed psycho-educational evaluations for approximately 3,500 kids. I also reviewed records for another 1,000-1,500 clients. In doing so, I believe I have been able to pull a lot of pieces together about cognition and diversity in learning that I have never seen written anywhere else. I have also been able to detail some of the complex relationships between language and visual information processing and describe the ways that sensory processing, intellectual performance, and differences in cognition all interact with one another.

Today, I teach part-time at the University of Northern Colorado in the Special Education department. I continue to offer assessments, advocacy, and consultation in my private practice as a school psychologist, and I sit on the U.S. Autism Advisory Board where I speak and train parents and educators at a national level. Across all these settings, I am frequently told that I understand cognition and neurodiversity better than most.

This story doesn't end here, though; there is at least one more chapter that evolved into this book. Eight years ago, I had a seizure while driving that caused a serious auto accident in which I broke my neck and partially severed my spinal cord. As a result, I had to spend the better part of a year in rehabilitation hospitals and physical therapy clinics. It was then that I made the decision to go back to school, and this time I had a specific research purpose.

INTRODUCTION

I wanted to deeply explore what had become my greatest passion in life: the topic of cognitive neurodiversity. To do this, I enrolled in a special education doctoral program (my first graduate degrees were in educational psychology and school psychology) with the intent of studying difference across the autism spectrum for my dissertation. I completed that doctorate in 2016, and the book you are about to read is drawn from that research. The dissertation was titled "First Person Perceptions: Intelligence, Cognition, and Sensory Processing in Autism," and if after reading this book you want to know more, you can access the original dissertation through most university libraries.

In the text that follows, I have condensed material from the dissertation and combined the findings of that research with my own impressions and thoughts. For clarity, the sections in grey boxes throughout this book are the actual, first-person accounts from the research participants; in regular font are my own thoughts and impressions. As an additional guide to you in your reading, I chose to use the general term "autism" throughout much of this text to denote the broad conditions of autism throughout various time periods, even when other terms or diagnostic labels were in use. The term autism spectrum disorder (ASD) has been reserved for discussions about current and future aspects of the condition. In my writing, I also tried to honor the individual by maintaining the use of "person-first language" (i.e., individuals with autism). However, within the words of those diagnosed, I felt it was not my place to change their language to adhere to person-first terminologies. Therefore, if the individual I was speaking to referred to him or herself (or to the group as a whole) as "autistics" or "Aspies," I left those terms in the text. After I considered this carefully, I decided it was more respectful to use the actual words given, rather than change the words of those diagnosed to adhere to current trends for "person-first language."

While all researchers probably feel like their work is in some way remarkable, I believe that what you are about to read is truly revolutionary in that it gives deep and meaningful insight into views on autism that have never been presented before. I have worked alongside those with ASD my entire career and have considered myself exceptionally well-read and well-trained in autism, but what I learned from this study took my breath away at times for its new additions and contributions to even my own understanding. What follows will make you laugh, cry, and wonder about this thing we all call autism.

CHAPTER ONE

Nuts and Bolts:
The Research Behind
the Book

So, the frustration for us is what you are trying to do. Take this for what it is, I am going to pull a total "Aspie" card here, sometimes it is really hard for those of us on the spectrum to be interviewed and measured by someone who isn't one of us.

With very few accounts about autism by those affected in the literature, and with the majority of my own opinions and thoughts about autism coming from my training, my life, and from the insights of my private practice clients, I made the decision to deeply explore the life experiences of seventeen adults who had been diagnosed with an autism spectrum disorder. The study took me approximately eighteen months, with six months of that time spent simply conducting interviews. It took another six months to compile and transcribe conversations and emails, going back and forth with the study's volunteers to find themes and trends. After I finally came to a place where I felt I understood what I had been told and was able to incorporate all of the essential words, ideas, and stories into a single text narrative, I worked with those in the study to construct a model that best encapsulated their responses. Last, I summarized the impressions and findings of my process, sharing my results with three expert professionals (individuals diagnosed with autism who work in the field of autism) to determine if they felt I had adequately captured the core features of autism, and to make additional revisions to the final conclusions.

A Qualitative Research Method

I specifically chose a research method that would allow me to deeply understand detailed aspects about neurodiversity. More than anything, I wanted an insiders' perspective on cognitive difference and neurodiversity in autism. The study method I selected specifically allowed me the time and opportunity to deeply get to know the people in the study. For those who care about such things, the research technique I used is referred to as a grounded-theory methodology. As a qualitative research method, the study was interpreted within a lens of social constructivism. This simply means that I spent a lot of time talking to and discussing the research topics with the volunteers, then working with them collaboratively to compile their words alongside my own and ground a theory. Or in other words, to form what I believe to be a new and truly revolutionary cognitive-behavioral model to explain core differences in autism.

The People in the Study

Now let me tell you a little bit about the individuals who volunteered to share their time and personal insights to create this work. This included fourteen adults who had been diagnosed somewhere along the autism spectrum (from various walks of life), along with three expert professionals who—while also diagnosed—had chosen as their life's work to speak and train others professionally on the topic of autism. Everyone who participated in the study was recruited from professional autism networks, social media pages, and from my own affiliation within the U.S. Autism Association.

Of the seventeen individuals that volunteered to help with the study, twelve were men and five were women. Their ages ranged between twenty-one and sixty-three. These people joined the study from twelve different states within the United States, and from three countries outside of the U.S. (Ireland, Morocco, and Australia). While all were diagnosed with an autism spectrum disorder (ASD), several had also been diagnosed with other physical or medical conditions and/or learning disabilities. The most obviously impaired individual in the study was a young woman who, in addition to her autism, has been blind since birth. While her disability was the most visibly recognizable, other severely disabling aspects of disability were reported by more than half of the volunteers.

While getting to know the people in the study, I learned that of seventeen total participants, fourteen were diagnosed to be on the autism spectrum as children; the remaining three had been diagnosed as teenagers or adults. Ten of the seventeen were diagnosed with Asperger's syndrome, five were diagnosed with *classical* autism and two were diagnosed with pervasive developmental disorders - not otherwise specified (PDD-NOS). All were now considered to be "higher functioning" and, not surprisingly, the diagnoses of Asperger's syndrome vs. autism closely aligned with the years in which the respective diagnoses were given.

Four of the men in the study had been very "low functioning" as children, and two of these didn't speak until they were eight or nine years old. Two others in the study still don't formally speak much as adults. Of the older members (over the age of forty-five), three of five had been referred as children for permanent institutionalization, even though they were quite "high functioning" later in life. One of the expert professionals, a college professor with a doctoral degree, was among the individuals who had been recommended as a child for placement into an institution.

Those in the study were at varying stages in their educations, careers, or vocations and three identified themselves as permanently disabled, although two of these individuals held part-time jobs (only one person in the study was considered permanently disabled to the degree that he could not work). Their vocational ranges were wide and included individuals with entry-level employment and/or educational pursuits (a full-time student, a food-service attendant, a telephone marketing operator, an airline stewardess, and an in-home health care provider); while advanced training careers such as computer programmer, professional photographer, university professor, and professional speaker and lecturer were reported for others. One individual in the study even held a high-level position within Foreign Affairs for the United States Government.

For the three individuals considered to be expert professionals, all had published books and written articles, regularly speaking and conducting autism-specific trainings at regional and national conferences. Within discussions about careers and vocations, it was interesting to note that several of the participants in the study reported holding higher-level or higher-paying positions in their past, but over the years had been forced to resort to work in lower-level, or even entry-level positions for long-term health and "sustainability."

Three of the members of this group held doctoral degrees, four had master's degrees or additional training beyond a four-year college degree, five were working on or had completed a bachelor's degree, and the remainder were high school graduates (although the youngest and essentially only true "non-vocal" member of the group had graduated from high school with significant modifications to his school curriculum).

Of the seventeen people, four were married (one now divorced) and three had children. One individual had married a woman diagnosed with obsessive-compulsive disorder and as a couple they had offered foster care to over a dozen disabled children, some of whom they had adopted. The rest of the group had chosen to remain single, and three lived with either parents or siblings.

The study included one person who identified as transgendered (female to male) and one individual who reported that he was homosexual. Because gender identity and sexual orientation were not specifically addressed unless the research participant brought them up, information about these topics for the remainder of those in the study isn't known.

Only two of the participants considered themselves essentially unable to speak. The expert professional who considered himself "non-verbal" actually could speak but did so only when he felt well rested, and only on "important enough occasions" (in hearing him speak, his speech was clearly slow and very labor intensive). The other non-verbal participant had, according to his speech therapist, less than 100 words in his actual spoken vocabulary (I am pleased to say that my name, Marlo, is now on his very short list). Both non-verbal individuals in the study were clearly capable of verbal thought, however, as both had written books. The expert professional used a keyboard for nearly all communication, while the young man required the assistance of an augmentative communication device and some minimal (no physical contact) prompting from his therapist or mother to assist him with most of his written communication.

The Research Procedures

The study itself was completed through multiple lengthy, in-depth interviews by telephone, computer conferencing technologies, or through online chat or e-mail exchange. All conversations, oral and written, were transcribed into text and without tying identities to statements. A transcript of all communications was compiled into a single text document. From there, using search features and a word frequency tool, I combed the transcript, looked for key words, grouped these, then chunked the groups into related sections with primary and secondary topics for each. At one point, I had over 2,000 pages of type-written text! I then revised sections, combined ideas, talked to everyone again, and after even more time together, I arrived at fifty-two different sets of original topics. The list that came out of this initial sorting process, organized in alphabetical order, follows:

anxiety and stress; attention, concentration, and focus; interests and perseverations; auditory processing and communication; behavioral control; bullying; cognition, cognitive strengths, cognitive challenges, and cognitive energy; cognitive theories (alignment with); compensation and coping; consistency and change; coordination; diagnosis; discrimination; difference and information processing; environment; executive functioning and multi-tasking; giftedness; higher education; injured autistic; information processing; intelligence and its measurement; interventions and supports; languages, English, learning a foreign language; learning (core academic subjects); lighting, memory, non-verbal communication; object permanence; processing speed; performance; safety; social interaction; social compliance and group dynamics; school experiences; sensory processing difference and effects on performance; sexuality; sound sensitivity, awareness of sounds and pitch; standardized tests; synesthesia; teachers; time; taste and smell; touch and texture; us and them; visual differences, strengths and challenges; vocations and employment; whole person; wisdom and discernment

Once I had this long list and had sorted it with the associated thoughts and ideas, I began to synthesize the text. I did this by going back through the list and continuing to talk to the volunteers until I believed I could finally make sense of everything I had been told and had figured out a method to sort and articulate it. From there, using SmartArt images to help me organize, I took the individual thoughts, ideas, transcribed sentences, and even combined paragraphs and organized these into primary groups. This gave me five initial topics that included: (1) sensory, (2) memory, (3) focus, (4) cognitive difference, and (5) social influence. Condensed further, these became the *theory of sensory-cognitive difference*. Before I introduce you to this new theory, I need to offer a short summary about what actually is within our current and collective understanding about autism, that is, what the existing theories have to say. To do this, I will briefly summarize the existing cognitive-behavioral theories and the primary assumptions about autism that have come out of the cognitive-behavioral tradition since autism was first reported in the clinical literature.

CHAPTER TWO

Understanding Autism
from the Cognitive
Behavioral Tradition

Until I was older, I didn't really know that I was different; well, I guess I knew I was different, but I just didn't think it was a difference that made a difference. It never dawned on me that my difference was a problem, because the differences I saw in others were not a problem for me.

Within society's accepted definitions for concepts about intelligence, disability, and developmental delay, we equate *difference* with *deficit*. This difference-as-deficit mindset has led to several cognitive-behavioral theories that have attempted to explain the core cognitive differences in autism while promoting various ways to "fix" or address the condition in those who are diagnosed. To fully understand this book and the reason for the proposal of a new cognitive-behavioral theory, which I call the theory of sensory-cognitive difference, we need to take a brief look at what existing cognitive-behavioral theories have had to say about autism through the years.

The Birth of Empirical Thinking

First, let me set the stage for the emergence of all existing cognitive behavioral theories that are accepted today as the "truth" about autism. We must go back to the year 1620, when Sir Francis Bacon openly contradicted Aristotle's claim that all things can be deduced through observation and human intuition. Bacon argued that we could not know the truth about the nature of things without a neutral, unbiased, and inductive method that begins with slow, careful, repeated observations applied and systematically measured within specific cases. For all of the sciences, this was the birth of empiricism, and as it is related to understanding the human mind, it meant we must deeply examine all things, case-by-case, to reach scientific consensus.

Wilhelm Wundt took Bacon's ideas a step further when he applied the emerging concept of reductionism (breaking things down into their most basic parts for observational purposes) to the understanding of human consciousness. This gave us as a society the belief that the mind, like a highly sophisticated machine, could be (at least conceptually, if not literally) taken apart and understood.

With this idea stacking up nicely alongside the full-blown industrial revolution of the late 1800s and early 1900s, dissection of the brain for the study of difference began in earnest. It was Jean Piaget (who only a short decade before Kanner and Asperger published the first accounts of autism in the scientific literature) that truly set the stage for the field of science to view autism as a developmental disability. In 1936, Piaget published a groundbreaking paper on the topic of human development and in it claimed that "normal development" was the foundation and basis for all intelligence. Piaget added that the emergence of intelligence—and thus cognition—in children could be traced back, reduced, and observed by specifically noting the ages in which a child progressed through several distinct and "normal developmental stages." This meant that before autism was ever formally written up as a disabling condition, the "normal" progression theory had become our way of thinking, and our collective views on *normal* and *developmentally appropriate* were virtually set in stone.

Autism and the Early Behaviorists

Then came autism as Leo Kanner suggested. Perhaps had history not so firmly placed neurotypical humans at the center of the universe just prior to the "discovery" of autism, the conditions of autism might have been viewed differently from the beginning. But that isn't what happened. Instead, as a society, we had firmly arrived at the belief that "normal" was best and that normal development occurred within certain distinct stages. This meant anything outside of normal was abnormal, and therefore problematic.

Without officially saying as much, this carried with it the implication that those conducting research on difference were themselves "normal" (or at least not developmentally abnormal) and that by comparing abnormal individuals to their normal counterparts in terms of development, we could rank, order, and understand all things related to intelligence and cognition in children. Within this worldview, we also fully accepted that human thinking could be observed, classified, categorized, measured, and reduced into several observable and teachable characteristics.

Because IQ tests were also aligned with these beliefs and had been developed during this same period in history to assess and predict global cognitive functioning, there was also the belief that intelligence, and thus cognition, could and should be routinely evaluated through standardized tests.

In turn, this resulted in the groundbreaking work of respected and "great" men like John B. Watson and B.F. Skinner (yes, a hint of cynicism can be assumed), who firmly believed that all human thought could be developed out of a "black box." This meant that human consciousness could not only be observed and fully understood, but difference could be identified, trained, and corrected through the application of specific behavior modification principles that are still today referred to as operant conditioning.

Given the predominantly factory-production view about education and learning of the time, combined with the developmental view of Piaget and the beliefs of the early behaviorists, language, communication, social, and behavioral skills such as sitting still in a chair, responding to directions, and giving the appearance of paying attention (after all, who can really assess if someone is actually paying attention?) became the primary focus for understanding and treating ASD.

But, this long line of thinking about thinking and naming others who are different as disabled and in need of behavioral change sets the stage for an understanding about autism that may or may not have been accurate. In other words, the beliefs of the day drove how we interpreted all the strengths and cognitive differences that were presented about the conditions of autism from the beginning. The heavy focus on deficits and developmental differences in autism completely ignored the prodigious memory, cognitive brilliance, and family histories from "highly intelligent stock" that both Kanner and Asperger had described in their original papers. This was true even though multiple reports about individuals who likely had autism long before Kanner and Asperger published had been written up in newspapers and scientific journals for decades earlier under the topics of "oddity or genius."

Early Attempts to Explain Autism

Developmental world views even led Bettleheim to claim that autism was caused by "cold refrigerator mothers." Although now entirely debunked, Bettleheim's theory suggested that because Kanner had reported that the mothers of these children were "highly intelligent," and many held teaching or research positions at universities, their work outside of the home had caused the children's autism. Remember, this was a time when most moms didn't work outside of the home, but instead ran the house and raised the children. So, with no additional data of his own, Bettleheim claimed that the children Kanner had written about suffered from arrested development due to "cold refrigerator mothering."

Luckily, this theory was fully dismissed after only a few years, but its impact lingered on; by then, the history of high intelligence in the families of these children had been dismissed as somewhat of a taboo topic, and the search was on for an explanation theory that was able to accurately describe the "developmental delays and differences" reported for those diagnosed with the condition of autism—specifically, from a behavior- and deficit-based perspective.

With this mindset as the starting place, the behaviorists, and later the cognitive-behaviorists, have arrived at several widely held conclusions about autism. These are referred to as cognitive-behavioral theories. Of the primary and distinct theories there are four, although modern thought about these explanations for autism generally accepts pieces and parts from each.

Theory of Mind Blindness

The first, and probably still most widely accepted, of the cognitive-behavioral theories was originally drawn from Descartes' writings about theory of mind, or the concept of thinking about thinking, as proposed in his book *Second Meditation*. Using this as their starting place, researchers in the field of autism concluded that those with autism lack theory of mind and therefore suffer from what we still call today a condition of "mind-blindness." This theory of mind idea, as originally put forth by Baron-Cohen, Leslie, Happé, and Frith in 1994, claims that individuals with autism fail to "impute mental states to themselves and others" and, as a result, show significant social deficits.

The mind-blindness theory was tested by numerous researchers through various play-based experiments, and based on the responses of those with autism, mind-blindness was diagnosed. One of the most famous tactics to evaluate a child for mind-blindness was a task in which children were asked to describe how a series of movements between geometrically shaped blocks occurred. Children with and without autism were then compared. Over many different subjects, neurotypical children more often responded with something like this:

What happened was that the larger triangle—which was like a bigger kid or bully—had isolated himself from everything else until two new kids come along, then the little one joined who was a bit more shy, and scared, so the smaller triangle more likely stood up for himself and protected the little one.

In contrast, those with autism more typically responded with something like this:

The big triangle went into the rectangle. There was a small triangle and a circle. The big triangle went out. The shapes bounced off each other. The small circle went inside the rectangle. The big triangle was in the box with the circle. Then the small triangle and the circle went around each other a few times (Klin, 2000, 840).

Researchers studying these different play sequences attributed them to what they called "inherent social generalization." Even now, the whole thing makes me laugh out loud—of course kids with autism will describe exactly what they see! Anyone who has ever worked with a child with autism knows this to be true. But does that really mean they are mind-blind or can't think about their own thinking? The theory claimed that normal children automatically assign feelings and emotions to non-human objects (which the researchers called social generalization). I suspect that part is true. The theory adds that "social generalization is impaired or not present for those with autism." I believe even this might be true. But, with these ideas in place, the theory concluded that those with autism are simply unable to understand or interpret human emotions within themselves or in others. This last part is the part that doesn't resonate with me, based on the individuals with autism that I have known.

While many people to this day still support the mind-blindness theory, and "gold standard" autism tests are based on mind-blindness, other researchers—including some of the same people who proposed theory of mind (Frith and Baron-Cohen in particular)—have since disputed it to varying degrees and within the research community. Some have even referred to mind blindness as a "folk theory." With less-than-universal acceptance, researchers moved on to find a different explanation that could more fully capture all the primary cognitive deficits seen in individuals with autism.

Executive Functioning Theory

Also in the early '90s, the disorder of executive functioning theory was proposed. This drew from older theories on something called "dysexecutive syndrome," which suggested that tasks of organizing, sequencing, and executing were impaired in individuals who had sustained traumatic brain injuries. In this theory, researchers Ozonoff and Rogers proposed that individuals with autism spectrum disorders have specific frontal lobe damage and, like other brain-injured populations, this causes them to need sameness, have difficulty in switching attention, and explains the tendency to perseverate; the theory also gave reasons for what they saw in ASD as a lack of impulse control.

To assess and treat executive functioning, researchers examined the skills of inhibition, intentionality, and executive memory and found that many individuals with autism and Asperger's syndrome (both conditions are now referred to as autism spectrum disorders or ASD) did have poor performance on certain aspects of executive functioning. But researchers attempting to prove the executive functioning theory didn't always find poor inhibition (impulse control) in those with ASD, which is almost always low in other groups with executive functioning disorders and is considered to be a key feature of the dysexecutive syndrome.

While this certainly threw a wrench into the theory of executive functioning for a time, the fact was that the impulse control piece seemed to be missing from the research findings. For many with ASD, the missing piece was eventually passed over as comparisons were made to those with and without impulse control problems in the attention deficit disorders. Today, the executive functioning theory is also still widely accepted and aspects of it are used regularly to address organizational needs, in particular for those with ASD. Having suffered from a brain injury myself, I can certainly attest to the effects of frontal lobe injury and subsequent interference with all of the tasks of executive functioning. But for me, this theory didn't explain how sensory overload contributes to dysexecutive syndrome. Just as I was unsatisfied with this explanation, so were researchers in the field. This led to several hybrid theories and a theory that eventually included sensory processing.

Hybrid Theories

With findings from the first two theories that were still inconsistent and inconclusive, researchers called for a hybrid theory between executive functioning theory and mind blindness because, as it was argued, executive functioning is "central to theory of mind." Still striving to find a cognitive processing difference theory that fully explained ASD, a third cognitive theory, the weak central coherence theory, was proposed. The weak central coherence theory was especially interesting to me because while it was still focused primarily on cognitive deficits, strong repetitive behaviors and preference for sameness were highlighted to explain the possibility for a "different cognitive-processing style."

This theory, too, was tested by measuring performance on certain tasks such as the Wechsler block design subtest, under the assumption that scores on these tests could predict strengths for abstract visual reasoning, segmentation, and attention to visual detail for those with ASD. Those who supported the weak central coherence theory explained it this way: the skill of *systemizing*—described elsewhere as visual sequencing, logic, and part-to-whole visual processing—presents as a global area of strength for individuals with ASD.

But this, too, could not be proven conclusively and from personal experience, I think I know why. Most of the tests used to assess the skills of systemizing are timed; some require specific motor planning skills (such as the block design subtest), and many individuals with autism react differently to these assessment tools than would otherwise be expected. For example, I have seen numerous individuals with autism complete several of the simpler items on the block design subtest in their exact mirror image. I have no idea why they do this, but I have also observed this to occur in certain individuals with dyslexia. So, when we compare the performance of a child with autism to that of a neurotypical kid, the strengths that are obvious to me as an evaluator are often lost in scoring. This is true even though I see and "sense" unusual, strength-based responses. I should probably mention here that I have personally evaluated approximately 3,500 children, many who came to me because their parents or teachers viewed them as twice-exceptional. Suffice it to say, my observational lens for unusual patterns of responding is wide. I believe that even though deep abstract visual and perceptual skills might be strong for many kids with autism, the tests we use to evaluate strengths in these areas too often get wiped out by other competing variables. I suspect this problem also interfered with the proof of the theory.

With non-conclusive results and a feeling that the weak central coherence theory might have focused too heavily on cognitive and strength-based differences in ASD, while failing to identify the challenges that were suggested through theory of mind or mind-blindness theory (primarily that of being able to empathize with others emotionally), the cognitive-behavioral researchers studying autism eventually combined the mind-blindness theory with the weak central coherence theory to put forth an *empathising-systemising theory*. The only difference here was that this new hybrid theory combined a few general strength areas in visual and cognitive processing differences while adding the component of deficit for empathizing. In effect, this theory became the "catch-all" for the previous theories.

Hyper-Systemizing Theory

Believing that none of the existing cognitive behavioral theories properly addressed significant sensory processing differences that he saw in autism, Baron-Cohen eventually proposed the fourth of the primary theories; he called his theory the *hyper-systemizing theory*. This theory came out shortly after Happé published her *empathizing-systemizing theory*. Baron-Cohen argued that ASD occurs primarily in children who are highly intelligent but also have significant sensory processing difference that makes them unable to sort, filter, and/or select a single set of information. According to this theory, sensory overload then *freezes* all other information processing. Hurray for Baron-Cohen! Given my own sensory challenges from head trauma and my experience in working with gifted children, this theory became the closest explanation I had studied and read about that seemed to explain what I felt to be a core aspect to the condition of autism. But, the Baron-Cohen theory was met with both acceptance and criticism. I also believe it had an additional problem with becoming mainstream—research to confirm the therapeutic benefits of occupational therapy, which seemed to be the logical treatment for autism based on the Baron-Cohen proposal, had not borne fruit in the clinical literature. By this point in time, the cognitive neurosciences were also taking center stage, and I believe these two elements made the Baron-Cohen theory less well known.

Autism and the Neurosciences

By the late 1990s, the cognitive neurosciences had taken the spotlight in attempts to explain autism. The brain differences of a person with autism, as it appeared on various scans, became the new "rabbit in the bush" for researchers to chase down in finding a cause and cure for autism. This meant that the tradition of attempting to explain autism through the field of cognitive-behavior sciences had grown cold, even though no theory as of yet arrived at agreement or consensus.

To date, none of the proposed cognitive-behavioral theories have been accepted universally and most new research primarily focuses on finding key anatomical and/or neurochemical differences that can explain the condition of autism. While many interesting anomalies and difference have been found in the past decade in particular, unfortunately, findings from the field of neurosciences have not gotten those who work with children who have autism any closer to understanding the core cognitive differences that could help them teach and direct learning for these children.

As both an educator and mental health clinician, it often feels like we, as professionals, are in the dark about what to do to help these kids. While we wait patiently for the next "big find" to come along, and more and more deficit-based topics emerge, the individuals who work with these kids day in and day out are primarily stuck with the existing theories. In both education and mental health, we don't even know what cognition really looks like for individuals with ASD. This leaves us with clinical research that only supports classical behavioral intervention strategies (ABA therapy) as our sole course and directive to address the complex needs of these children!

Some researchers and clinicians are now proposing that one day soon, autism could become a medical condition, as we begin to more fully understand the human genome and some of the "loading" theories that have physically interfered with normal development for these kids. It should also be noted that the field of neuroscience has been heavily criticized by those with autism for being overly reductionistic and failing to look at autism from the standpoint of what those with the condition can do, and what they need from us to be successful in school and in the workplace.

The Neurodiversity Movement

This has led to a new movement driven by various groups, including those with autism. Referred to as the theory of neurodiversity, a new trend suggests that perhaps we, as a society, should abandon the search for defining and fixing differences in autism (and all neurocognitive differences for that matter) and instead embrace the idea that no theory should try to explain or treat autism, because those on the autism spectrum simply have a different way of doing things and this difference should be respected and honored.

Breaking entirely with the cognitive-behavioral tradition and even somewhat with the long line of thinking about developmental difference that essentially drives the cognitive neurosciences, the neurodiversity movement has certainly gained momentum. But, for many with autism, the neurodiversity movement feels "empty" and devoid of any explanation or means to garner support for the very real and disabling aspects of living with autism. People working with individuals with autism also argue that neurodiversity, while nice in theory, leaves little to no insight or explanation that is actually *helpful* to professionals and educators who wish to become better trained and knowledgeable in their support for those who struggle with aspects of their autism. In my own opinion, the neurodiversity movement also leaves little room to improve diagnostic accuracy or support for children or families impacted by the more severe and disabling aspects of autism. Finally, according to those who criticize neurodiversity from the medical community, the neurodiversity movement doesn't help at all when a child is truly disabled and made ill by their condition, as is the case for many children with autism who suffer from debilitating stomach issues or bravely tolerate thousands of seizures a year.

Introducing the Theory of Sensory-Cognitive Difference

So, here we are. While everyone agrees that both cognitive and sensory differences are present in ASD, we are left in the crosshairs between the proponents of the current neurodiversity movement and the existing (albeit still limited) cognitive-behavioral theories from that past that don't really tell us what autism is or how we should address it clinically or in the classroom. As such, I believe this leaves a huge gap in the middle for what is now needed: a much richer, deeper, and more complete cognitive-behavioral theory about difference in autism, built from the insights of those diagnosed.

It is clear to me that any new theories about autism should both honor neurodiversity from the standpoint of strength-based contributions, while still recognizing and supporting the differences and needs that matter and are in some way problematic for individuals with ASD. So, there you have it in a nutshell. The proposed theory that follows and how it emerged is exactly what the rest of this book is about. In the chapters that follow, I will walk you through what I discovered in my conversations with those with autism and, hopefully, by the time you finish, you will arrive with me at an understanding about the need for and value of an entirely new cognitive-behavioral theory that I call the theory of *sensory-cognitive difference*.

I also hope that you will see, as I do, the profound implications that I think this new theory holds for improving the lives of those diagnosed and for assisting those who have the privilege of walking beside someone with ASD. This new theory, the *theory of sensory-cognitive difference*, is both aligned with and contrasted against existing theories and is set against the backdrop of the emerging neurodiversity movement. Built from the thoughts of those diagnosed instead of professionals who often don't have a "different mind" themselves, I believe you will see that this theory is more accurate and complete than any in existence.

Cognition and the Birth of Sensory Processing Theory

As the very first step to understanding this new theory, I will need you to first step outside of your historical paradigm of "developmentally normal" and traditional empirical thinking to consider a very different world view than the one I have detailed above. Originating out of the complex work of Dr. Charles Sherrington, the father of modern-day neuropsychology, I would next like to introduce you to Dr. Jane Ayers and her *theory of sensory processing*. I do this because, in my opinion, the first step to understanding the *theory of sensory-*

cognitive difference is fully reconsidering the complexities of our truly magnificent sensory and neurophysiological processing systems.

CHAPTER THREE

A Different Approach: Sensory Processing Theory

23

The brain is like a sparkling field of rhythmic flashing points with trains of traveling sparks hurrying hither and thither... it is as if the Milky Way entered in upon itself in some cosmic dance, becoming an enchanted loom, where millions of flashing shuttles weave a dissolving pattern, always a meaningful pattern though never an abiding one; a shifting harmony of subpatterns. (Sir Charles Sherrington, 1942, Man on his Nature)

By the early 60s, while most of the world had gotten on board with the idea that all aspects of cognition could be broken down and systematically observed, just as simply as one could take apart a watch to see how it worked, neuropsychologist Dr. Jean Ayers thought differently. Drawing from the work of Sir Charles Sherrington, the father of modern-day neuropsychology, Dr. Ayers offered a different and even contradictory look at development, cognition, and intelligence by claiming that in spite of one's development, *normal performance* could only occur in the presence of a normally functioning sensory processing system. Ayers claimed that the complex neurophysiological job of the sensory processing system allowed individuals to successfully access, integrate, filter, process, organize, and act on the information that is present within the external world. But unlike the linear and reductionistic view of her colleagues, Ayers added "normal" functioning within the sensory processing system (not the attainment of developmental milestones) underlies all cognition, at the most basic level, because the system of sensory processing serves as the sole interface between the body and world.

The Complexity of the Sensory Processing System

In the field of autism, while numerous studies have shown that significant sensory processing differences exist for almost everyone diagnosed, very little is still actually known about how sensory processing differences manifest, affect functioning, or impact one's developmental trajectory.

According to Ayers, to understand sensory processing (especially for its implications in ASD, although Dr. Ayers' theory was never specific to autism), we must first shift our ideas and beliefs about the topics of thinking and cognition. Dr. Ayers tells us that the tasks of sensing, perceiving, organizing information, remembering, and performing do not occur in linear sequences and the components that make up these processes are not distinct. The mind-body interface system that we refer to as the sensory processing system must work continuously and in constant relationship to all other parts of peripheral and central nervous systems, both from the inside out as well as from the outside in.

For this reason, sensory processing cannot be systematically observed, measured, or targeted for change through formal operant conditioning methods. More specifically, because every aspect of sensory processing occurs all the time and exists under the very broad umbrella of cognitive processing, sensory processing is simply far too complex for us to properly reduce, analyze, or treat.

By 1972, Ayers clearly seemed to understand that certain individuals struggle with the innate neurological process that organizes sensations from their bodies and from the environment, making it difficult or impossible to use the body "normally" or even effectively within the environment. For Ayres, this meant that all learning and performance will be negatively affected if some neural function causes the inability to integrate and regulate incoming information (in other words, if one cannot accurately process and organize information coming in from the world around them, they will be unable to act on it or learn from it). Ayers' sensory processing theory included discussions about the five primary senses (touch, sound, sight, taste, and smell), but also incorporated the sensations of movement and pressure into the theory.

Sensory Theories Debunked and Revisited

Unfortunately, in the years that followed, Ayers' theory was largely discredited by the scientific community. From the beginning, doctor Ayers had proposed that children benefit from exposure to specific sensory experiences that engage the central nervous system. In her work, she virtually created the field of occupational therapy as it relates to sensory processing disorders in children. But, when clinical trials attempted to measure the effectiveness of sensory processing therapy, the methods themselves could not be clinically supported in the literature. Unfortunately, this caused the medical community as well as many mental health clinicians, researchers, and educators to essentially discredit all of Dr. Ayers' work. This was true even though parents by the hundreds of thousands continued to flock to occupational therapists for the treatment of sensory differences in their children, often reporting significant improvements in their children and paying for therapies at their own expense.

Once again, we see that the prevailing empirical, developmental, and linear world views held the topic of "difference" hostage as it related to the work of Dr. Ayers, and the families of ASD children who genuinely reported benefit (even though these benefits could not be fully measured) were unable to prove the benefits they knew they saw. In the actual dissertation that is the foundation for this book, I spent considerable time reviewing the reports of families who saw benefits from occupational therapy for their ASD children and found these claims weren't happenstance or reported in only a handful of cases. Hundreds of thousands of people made claims that occupational therapy was, in fact, beneficial.

Perhaps more than any other point along this entire journey, I came to the full realization that, in spite of what most people *feel*, *believe*, or *know* to be true, unless things can bear out in randomized clinical trials, they will be completely discredited. But, who in education or clinical practice has the millions of dollars necessary to conduct a clinical trial on something that doesn't make millions in return?

Luckily, for reasons that are only now beginning to resurface in the field of neuroscience, more accurate scanning and examination tools can now essentially "see" brain activity as the nervous system interacts with sensory inputs from the environment. Some are finally beginning to wonder if Ayres' original theory may still be the most accurate to date regarding sensory processing and learning in autism. It is also true within the field of neuroscience that the more we think we understand about autism, the more we realize there is yet to be understood. I fully believe in and support the theory behind Jean Ayers' work, even though some of the occupational therapy techniques may or may not work for all children.

About twenty years ago, before the work of occupational therapy had been clinically discredited, it was common practice to brush all children who struggled with sensory processing disorders with a soft-tooth, medical-grade scrub brush. The brushing technique was studied clinically, and children were placed on "brushing schedules," then behaviors such as paying attention, finishing work, and the like were tracked and measured. I remember those years well, because while some children loved to be brushed, from the perspective of the majority of the kids with autism that I saw, brushing was their hell!

This failed research methodology, in particular, made me realize that not only is the sensory system far more complex than we can possibly imagine (as Ayers stated), it is also highly specialized and unique for each individual. I guess we shouldn't wonder, then, why one sensory stimulation method, applied liberally across a broad range of observed sensory differences in children, did not bear out clinically.

I should add that it was within these years that I came to equate sensory processing from the standpoint of the swing on a pendulum: each of our individual sensory experiences can be either over-stimulated or under-stimulated in any single moment (and this does not mean that they all line up, because the auditory system could be an overload while the visual system is under stimulated). These experiences are directly affected by how tired or bored we are at any point in time. I even created a model explaining these relationships that has since been widely adopted.

Additional Sensory Processing Topics Specific to My Research

For the topics of my research, I found it especially interesting to note that Ayers reported a much higher frequency of sensory processing impairment and difference in children with learning disabilities and cognitive learning style differences. Even more specific to my research, Ayers added that at the bottom of the intellectual bell curve (based on IQ scores), children with cognitive disabilities, such as Down's syndrome, struggle more than other children to accurately process sensory information. Ayers added that sensory challenges for low-IQ children most often take the form of poor or inaccurate sensory integration (an inability to register the correct signal). But at the high end of the intellectual bell curve, while sensory processing differences are also quite common in those who are intellectually gifted, sensory differences tend instead to have a greater impact on filtering, modulation, and attention (an inability to use the signal received correctly).

This brought me to a statement that I hear often within the intellectually gifted community: "gifted kids process more information and, as such, they have the tendency to be more hyper-sensitive and over-excitable." Often referred to as the "Normal Sensitivities and Over-Excitabilities of Gifted Children," Kazimierz Dabrowski (a researcher specializing with gifted children) hypothesized that differences in sensitivity were part and parcel to being intellectually gifted. What is missing, though, is enough research to clarify what sensory differences might look like for those with ASD.

Across the autism spectrum, we know that atypical sensory processing is reported in approximately 96 percent of diagnosed individuals. As such, it has become widely accepted (especially within the neurodiversity movement) that understanding sensory difference in ASD is a critical first step to tailoring appropriate and effective programs and treatments. Neurodiversity theory calls for honoring and attending to sensory difference (among other things), and in so doing, the neurodiversity movement applies the term "niche construction." Within neurodiversity, there is a premise that if an individual is appropriately honored and supported for their sensory and cognitive differences, a safe space opens up for individuals to function as optimally as is possible (creating a "niche" for optimal functioning and performance). In turn, neurodiversity adds that if a successful niche is created, successful functioning within a modified (or niche-constructed) environment results in the individual being able to expand their functioning in more neurotypical settings.

But even with compelling research coming out of the field of neurobiology and a call for attention to sensory needs within the neurodiversity movements, very little is still being done to understand or address sensory difference in ASD, especially within traditional learning or work environments. In my mind, and with my own sensory differences still playing largely in my life, I believe that this is due, at least in part, to the fact that we still lack a basic understanding about what sensory processing difference actually is or what it feels like for those along the autism spectrum.

Because our traditional methods of thinking and understanding cognition and behavior rely so heavily on empirical evidence, I was astounded to learn that in 800,000 studies on individuals with autism, only a few had seriously stopped to ask more than one or two people with autism about their own sensory processing experiences. In my mind, what better way is there to learn about sensory differences in autism than to ask those affected? So, that is exactly what I did. The chapter that follows details the first-person accounts of individuals in my study on the topic of sensory processing difference in autism.

CHAPTER FOUR

Sensory Difference:
Insights from Within

CHAPTER FOUR

I suspect that we literally think in specific sensations. I've noticed that autistic people are likely to describe specific sensory experiences they've had rather than the events that others might be focusing on.

For all the volunteers in my research, significant sensory differences had been or seemed to be a major factor of their autism. More specifically, only one person in this study did not believe he had very significant sensory processing differences or that sensory difference had shaped his life. Even for this individual, though, I had observed him to have what I felt could be some pretty specific sensory adaptations. For example, this person only ever wore roughly the same brand of pants, a logo t-shirt (sometimes with a sweater vest) and a baseball hat to every event, even when lecturing or attending a dinner party.

As I thought about this, I realized that—considering my own sensory changes from the accident—I, too, had some pretty specific clothing preferences of my own. Who among us doesn't, to some degree? In other words, I viewed my own funky clothing choices as okay (my mom even teases me about them, saying "you wear the damnedest things"), but his were odd and proof of his sensory processing disorder.

Certainly, then, my own sensory differences from my accident shaped how I looked at myself and others in relationship to sensory differences. Even with that aspect in mind, looking back through all of my years of practice, even before my own accident, I discovered that I could not remember meeting a single person diagnosed on the autism spectrum that didn't have something *quite* different going on in certain areas of their own sensory processing that was specifically attributed to their autism. While these were vastly different across individuals—some were extremely hypo-sensitive (tuned out) while others were hyper-sensitive to the degree that day-to-day functioning was painful—every individual with autism that I had ever known had specifically commented on sensory processing difference that impacted them in their daily lives. To me, this felt different than merely preferences about clothing.

Twice-Exceptional and ASD Kids Share the Same Sensory Differences

What was even more startling for me to realize, however, was the reason I hadn't noticed a specific trend before for sensory difference as an "autism-specific" trait. The twice-exceptional kids I had worked with, both intellectually gifted and disabled, all had some of what seemed like the same sensory processing differences as those with autism. I don't think I mentioned this before, but for about ten years I owned and operated a private school for children who were gifted but also struggled (in spite of their intellectual strengths) with learning, socialization, mental health, and/or behavior. In my school of about seventy-five students, only 25 percent were on the autism spectrum. In the beginning I wasn't sure these kids could work together, but the thing that surprised me most was when we addressed sensory needs for all kids. The kids with autism did well socially and, otherwise, placed with peers who were not on the spectrum. Moreover, everyone in the building required some significant adaptations and respect for differences in sensory modulation, while only a few of the kids in my school had true sensory integration disorders.

It was during this time that I came to realize Ayers had suggested that neurodiversity and high intelligence correlated to challenges with modulating sensory information. But what if for those with autism, both different-mindedness and high intelligence were present? Wouldn't that make these problems even more pronounced? Certainly, the kids with autism in my school were every bit as intelligent and sensitive as the other twice-exceptional kids in the building; though as a group, their overall IQ scores were not nearly as high.

People visiting the school often remarked on the fact that the school looked more like an occupational therapy clinic than a traditional learning environment. I don't think I had intended to do this when it opened, but as it progressed, I found that the more we attended to sensory needs, the better the kids did in other areas. Because of my own injuries, I intuitively knew what a lot of these kids needed, as these were the same things I needed. In a 7,500 square foot building, we had three "peace places" complete with dim lighting, comfortable chairs, and even foot baths for a time; an ever-active sensory gym with kick bags, a trampoline, a rocker board, spinners, and a climbing rope; open-door "time-out" booths in each room that were covered in carpet, contained several pillows, and held a can of multi-colored beans (for sorting to end the time out); at least a half-dozen sensory baskets containing fidgets, brushes, chew tubes, sour candies, aromatherapy scents, stretch toys, pencil grips, and weights; five small pop-up tents; a dozen weighted therapy balls; four weighted stuffed animal snakes that were eight feet long and weighed between twenty and forty pounds; a dozen or more body socks (stretchy, body-length tubes that allow kids to crawl inside); and enough noise-cancelling headphones for every child in the building to have their own pair. When we did sensory things right, our kids did well.

Here's what the individuals in my study had to say about their own sensory processing differences:

> It seems to me that the higher one's intelligence is, the more sensory information they are faced with. If intelligence is the process of making connections between ideas and solving problems, then having unusual sensory experiences might make a person seem unusually intelligent or creative.
>
> I think our differences in sensory processing can be likened to the differences between serial and parallel bus ports on a computer. A serial bus is like a single-lane road. If you had eight cars that were traveling together, they would have to form a single queue to pass that stretch of road and regroup again after passing it. I'm pretty sure neurotypicals (NTs) process in serial. But a parallel bus is like an eight-lane freeway. The same party of eight cars can travel its length eight abreast, if so inclined. I (and others like me) process in parallel. Using the model of a super-highway, during periods of hypo-sensation, a "lane" is effectively closed. Hyper-sensation would be analogous to an elevated speed limit in a given lane.

Sound Sensitivity

As I began to consider various sensory topic subcategories for this section, I was reminded about my own sensory processing differences. After my head injury, the world got very loud, seemingly overnight. I could no longer filter certain sounds and the thought of going out to dinner at a noisy restaurant gave me pain in my stomach. Also, I recalled that in the school I ran I had purchased fifty pairs of headphones, but because kids had taken them for use at home, we only had ten or fifteen pairs in the building by that first Christmas break.

As I started to comb the data for sensory differences that related to sound, I expected to see sound sensitivity that mirrored my own experiences and that of the kids in my school—and I did. At first glance, it appeared that sound sensitivity was one of the most severe of the sensory issues reported and some aspect of this affected everyone in my study. But what I didn't expect to find was that for some people with autism, the ability to engage in extreme *tuning out* (clinically referred to as hypo-responding) was present, too. So, while the majority of the study's volunteers reported significant issues with pain in their ears that were associated with certain sounds (fifteen out of seventeen), for the two who were hypo-sensitive (able to tune out), it seemed that the very same sounds that were painful were the ones that were completely absent or blocked out entirely.

As I explored this further, an interesting observation was shared by one of the participants: "*for those of us who are strong verbal facts people,*" i.e., those with a clear verbal learning style, "*our issues with sound tend to lean toward the ability to block things out.*" When I explored this topic with others, I learned that while they knew others with autism who could apparently tune out completely, their inability to block out sound was so severe that it had prevented them from being able to secure or maintain employment.

In addition to problems with sound, or an extreme ability to block out sound, three of the people in the study also specifically identified themselves as having perfect pitch. For one of these, this had led to a successful career in music with a PhD teaching music and music theory at a university. The actual word-for-word statements that came out of my search for the topic of sound sensitivity are highlighted below.

My worst area of sensitivity, by far, is sound. I literally have pain in my ears.

Certain noises really hurt. I remember experiencing a fire alarm where the pain of the sound seemed to start at my head and radiate all through my body.

I have heard others talk about hearing the Wi-Fi system, which has actually been documented, but in terms of some of these sense noises, I find them very distracting.

I didn't realize sound was a problem for me as I had always worked in quiet environments. But recently I have come to realize that my ability to deal with this is much poorer than other people.

If I can make a comparison, someone talking near to me is the equivalent of a light being shone into the eyes of an NT. It can't be blocked out or ignored and the effort required to overcome the distraction is very stressful and tiring. When this happens, my quality of work goes through the floor, which is deeply embarrassing.

I enjoy getting away from the city to a place where I can hear everything from very far away and nothing hurts my ears. Way back in primary school, my class was tested for auditory differentiation (telling two slightly different tones apart) and I got a perfect score. I have absolutely perfect pitch, which has been tested.

I believe that for some of us, our sound sensitivity issues caused so much pain that we are literally survivors of torture and react from the standpoint of something like post-traumatic stress disorder.

As it related to tuning out (hypo-responding) to sound, which was reported by only two of the participants in this study, the following comments were offered alongside insights about hypo-responding from others who experienced heightened sound sensitivity.

Loud noises don't bother me at all. I don't even hear certain sounds, or rather certain frequencies. I'm quite hypo-sensitive to high-pitched sounds and this actually causes significant issues with safety. My hypo-sensitivity to sound makes driving a bit dangerous because I might not hear an ambulance, a police car, or someone honking their horn at me.

I remember once the whole block was up in arms because my fire alarm was going off for several hours and, even though I was in there right under it, I didn't hear it. The police finally came and knocked on my door, asking me to turn it off, but I really didn't notice it.

I know lots of "verbal facts" people through autism and Asperger's support groups. They seem to be the types who are great at trivia, but they also seem—at least from what I can tell—to experience fewer sensory disturbances, especially for painful sounds. People who think primarily in words seem to experience less sensory issues. Please don't take this as fact, it's just an observation from my own experience.

I think that, for those of us with more advanced language abilities, we have learned to block certain aspects of our sensory responding to sound entirely. But when we tune out, it doesn't seem to be the same thing as the filtering or discriminating of sounds that others are able to do. When we tune out, we tune out entirely!

Lights and Colors

Because several of the participants paired light with sound, I initially thought about this category in line with the previous one as a sensitivity to a variety of visual assaults. But across my entire data set, I did not have a single person refer to any other visual sensory issue except for fluorescent lights, very bright LED lights, and for only one person in this group, bright fluorescent clothing.

In my own life, I have been made well-aware of problems that I face when forced to work under fluorescent lights. I also get dizzy and sick to my stomach with movement and even bright sunlight is a problem. The kids in my school also required significant adaptations to standard fluorescent lighting and, as any teacher can tell you, the room got quiet when we dimmed the lights. To this day, I can't tell you if my own experiences or the experiences of the twice-exceptional kids without autism were exactly the same as it was for those with autism. While auditory sensitivities seemed to be the same for both groups and for myself, sensitivity in the visual domain seemed different. Here's what those with ASD had to say about their visual sensitivities.

I am very sensitive to fluorescent lights, I can also hear them. Standing under bright fluorescent lights is not really within my skill set.

Lighting made a big impact on me when I was young, especially fluorescent lights. If I try now to work under fluorescent lights, I can't think, I can't concentrate, and I get overly tired.

The harshness of some lights is really, really painful for me. Certain lights still give me headaches. Flickering, blinking, or LED lights are physically painful, and I get pain behind my eyes from exposure to them.

Some of my sensory challenges have sort of changed as I have grown up, but my bat cave condo must still be kept very dark and quiet. I use little blue bulbs that give off just a minimum of light so that I can see what I am doing. Then, if I really need to see stuff, I will turn on a brighter light, but only for a minute. Then the lights have to go out again as soon as I'm finished.

I have a tremendous amount of awareness about color and light intensity. Sometimes colors within the spectrum of light are just too bright. I can also see the color temperature of lights, the pulsing frequencies of LEDs, fluorescent lights, sodium, mercury, and even tungsten when they start to fluctuate. For me, it's generally a good skill set because it is applicable to my career as a photographer, but for other things it is highly offensive. I simply cannot have an LED in my house because it becomes too painful for me.

I sometimes see people wearing those really bright fluorescent or neon t-shirts and I have to look away because if I look at them too long, they will give me a headache.

I have noticed that for those of us who are very visual in our minds, we are also more sensitive to visual things like lights. I think there is a different neural pathway system there for those of us on the spectrum.

As I have learned more about brain functionality, I have discovered that specific "modules" exist for processing different aspects of visual information and others for other sensory input. I think for those of us with autism, we literally have a different visual module.

I truly believe that, at least for some of us, our brains use the disparity between each eye to a great effect. For the verbal facts people, it seems they are usually less sensitive to visual things like blinking or fluorescent lights, and perhaps they have learned how to block out some of this competing information.

As was true in the area of sound, the same two people who had been able to block noise were also capable of using their "tuning out" skills to block out flickering or obtrusive fluorescent lights. But, in addition, one of the people who was highly sensitive to sound had little to no awareness or difficulty with lights. Here's what these three had to say.

I don't think I notice sounds or blinking lights, maybe I remember having some problems in these areas when I was younger, but I'm certainly able to tune them out now.

Lights don't bother me at all. Even though I know they are a problem for many people on the spectrum, I just don't notice them. I remember one time sitting in my office and the fluorescent bulb was blinking on and off for several days before it finally burned out. More than a few people asked me how I could stand it. I remember being kind of surprised by that because I really had not noticed the flickering bulb at all.

I guess I'm quite hyper-sensitive to things like fluorescent lights. People come into my office and ask, "Isn't that light driving you crazy?" I just tell them, "I didn't really notice it until now." Sometimes it's a problem, but mostly because it is a problem for others.

As I processed these responses against my own experiences, I recognized in myself that extreme sensitivity to light (and even occasional sensitivity to color) was quite apparent following my head injury. In fact, to this day, my eye doctor always adds another layer of color to my tinted prescription sunglasses. I even have glasses that tint to oncoming traffic for when I drive at night. I think I am less aware of these differences now, they are just a part of my new normal, but I do recall being only able to wear white or black shirts for about three years following my accident as prints or colors seemed to interfere with my vision in my peripheral field. I also could not drive at night for nearly five years after my accident because my pupils would not dilate quickly enough for me to see after passing a car with its headlights on. This had the effect of leaving me blind for two or three seconds after I passed every car. I explored my own experiences with some of the individuals in the study, particularly the individual who reported problems with color, and determined that even though the end result of my own light sensitivity might have felt the same, the actual experience did not seem to be. I learned that for individuals with autism, vision appears to be "highly aware" to a degree that my own vision is not, and for this reason, light sensitivity in ASD might come specifically from too much visual information processing.

Touch and Texture

Within the next sensory difference category, only about half of the respondents in the study chose to discuss differences with touch and texture, although I have observed this extensively in my work with ASD children and many of the children who attended my school. Following my accident, I also experienced unbearably sensitive skin. While the previous two categories had elicited a response in every one of the individuals in the study, I found that touch and texture had improved considerably for at least some of these volunteers since their childhoods, and they no longer felt this was a problem. For seven people in the study, touch sensations were still notably disrupted.

Those with significant touch disturbance reported that learning to understand disrupted touch sensations had helped them learn how to accept these differences. In so doing, two of the people in the study had learned, as adults, to associate light touch with pleasant touch. Distractions such as clothing tags or bumps in socks were mentioned by several as being particularly offensive and for one of the very hypo-sensitive participants, clothing issues were still a significant problem in adulthood to the degree that he could not wear normal clothing. The responses that stood out in this area are highlighted in the following paragraphs.

I often still experience touch in a strange way. I don't always only feel touched in the spot where I was touched. Someone will touch lightly or unpredictably and some of that sensation will travel throughout that side of my body.

Touch was really a problem when I was younger. The lighter the touch the more unpleasant it became, and I didn't always know where it came from so it confused and frightened me.

Touch for me was like nails on a chalkboard, except it was on my skin. But firmer, slower grips, like hugs, were generally okay.

Now that I finally understand what's happening to me, how different my sense of touch really is, the touch thing can be pleasant. A friend's light kiss on the cheek can feel like they caressed that entire side of my body with a large feather or a brush.

I still have to wear the right texture of clothes, natural, soft fabrics, and nothing too tight. When I was a kid, I could not stand that tag in my shirt, it was like somebody had a knife in me.

I know it bothered other people, but if the tag in my shirt or a bump in my sock was a problem for me, I had to take care of it that exact moment or I couldn't focus on anything else.

I can't easily wear clothes all day long and wearing clothes for more than a few days in a row just isn't possible. My skin is still just so sensitive that I have to wear a very specific robe when I am at home, or I wear nothing at all. Obviously, this keeps me indoors!

Food and Smell

Reports about texture, the pressure needed to chew, and taste in food was anomalous for about half of the people in the study. For some, eating had actually been at some point in their lives a safety issue, and yet others described eating as an exciting and interesting adventure. My own experiences had changed the ways that foods tasted and smelled, and I too had grown more sensitive; but unlike those with autism, I found that some new foods that I had not liked before now tasted good. Certainly, most of the ASD kids that I have known throughout my professional career have been described as "picky" eaters, but I have also known at least a dozen ASD kids who routinely ate non-food items to the degree that they had been diagnosed with pica. None of the individuals in the study commented on the topic of pica, and none had ever eaten non-food items.

Sensitivity to smell was also noted for a few of the volunteers and some of these also aligned with safety (the ability to use smell to gauge something as safe to eat). A few took the smell and taste questions I asked in other directions. Initially, I expected heightened sensitivity in these areas to line up with sensitivity that was reported in other areas. However, at least for those in this study, that did not appear to be true. The individuals with heightened sensitivity to lights or sounds were not necessarily the most sensitive to smells or tastes. In this group, the opposite even seemed true.

As I thought about this more, I came to realize that sensory differences in the areas of taste and smell (perhaps even more than sensory difference in other areas) confirmed my sensory processing model and verified that someone can be hyper-sensitive in one area while simultaneously being hypo-sensitive in another. As such, an individual cannot be described simply as a person who is either over or under responsive, because individuals might be "both" or "neither," and these might change to some degree in the moment. Thus, and still much like the swing of a pendulum that I described earlier, a person's sensory sensitivities, while following a general trend or pattern, can change significantly throughout the day based on the amount of cognitive energy the individual has to accurately filter and regulate the sensory responses.

The statements about tastes and foods from the individuals in this study aligned nicely with that theory and the exact statements to support it follow.

If I don't like a certain food, it is usually because of the texture. I am pretty limited by what I can eat as certain textures in food really bother me. To this day, I cannot eat bananas or avocados.

I sometimes surprise myself and enjoy certain strong-tasting foods. When I eat, I can pick up really subtle things in tastes that are fun an enjoyable, at times.

I don't seem to get overloaded by food like I did when I was young. I love all smells, even some of the stronger ones that other people describe as stinky, although I do notice that some days this isn't true.

When I was a kid, I remember the only meat that I felt like I could chew without choking was chicken nuggets. Everything else just took too much work to chew up and swallow. If I wasn't very careful about what I ate, I could literally choke.

To this day, I still prefer chicken nuggets to any other protein source. They are easy to look at—I have a hard time eating something where I can see blood or veins—the taste and texture are very predictable, and quite honestly, they're bland with no strong animal taste.

For about a decade, I lived almost exclusively on chicken nuggets and macaroni and cheese. This had to always be the same brand and cooked to the same consistency. If we went on vacation and my mom didn't bring those brands with her, or we couldn't get the consistency right because we might be cooking in the microwave for example, I truly could not eat.

In some instances, taste and smell were praised for their ability to keep some of the participants from eating something that was spoiled and for providing added value to recognition of places and people. One of the participants describes her ability to smell or eat stronger tasting foods in relationship to her level of fatigue. During a discussion about smells, one of the participants also volunteered on the topic of sexuality for its relationship to smell. Several of those in the study also referred to their enjoyment or displeasure when eating gained from heightened senses of taste and smell. The most interesting of these points are included below.

I've been told that my sense of smell is amazing. I tend to notice lots of different smells. I often recognize people and places just by their scents.

I am the first person to know the milk is going bad. Others will realize it a day or two later, but for me it is strong the moment it turns. My sniffer saves me from bad stuff going in my mouth.

Once, when I was a kid, my mom tried to put the cheap brand of ketchup into the good brand ketchup bottle. Before I even tasted it, I was sure it had gone bad. Then she started looking guilty, so I put it together.

I can be pretty darn sensitive when it comes to smells. There is an ebb and flow for taste and smell that is even more noticeable than it is for things like lights, sounds, or textures. I can't always predict how I'm going to react to a certain smell or taste. For example, there are days when I might be able to eat a piece of pizza with a little Parmesan on it and really enjoy it. Then there are other days when I have to leave the room because I can't even tolerate the Parmesan smell in the air.

My responses to taste and smell have a lot to do with the time of day and how taxed my mental state is. I'm generally much higher functioning earlier in the day when it comes to smells and tastes.

I think for many of us there are smell differences that affect us sexually; the physical, the olfactory, all the smells, it's awkward to have this conversation but I think we need to have this conversation.

I have remained celibate for my entire adult life because I just can't face all the smells and mixed sensations that are associated with sexuality. It's not that I don't have sexual urges, but I simply don't have a way to indulge them.

Synesthesia

Defined in the Merriam-Webster collegiate dictionary (2005) as a "concomitant sensation; especially a subjective sensation or image of a sense other than the one being stimulated," *synesthesia* was reported on several occasions by the individuals in this study. As a topic beneath the area of sensory processing difference, this was especially interesting to me, because I had also experienced a sort of synesthesia following my spinal cord injury. To this day, I still have some mixed sensations due to nerve damage; but as I explored this, I realized that mine are nothing like those with autism describe. While I feel cold instead of hot or lack sensation, I don't see or hear anything that is tied to my sense of touch. For some people with autism, synesthesia takes on an entirely different dimension than even I can't understand.

Additionally, one of the participants in the study was blind, and this provided a really interesting contribution because she had visual synesthesia for touch, even though she had never been able to see with her actual eyes. For her, a great deal of "visual imagery" still accompanied her sensory sensations.

By listening to the participants' words, I concluded that while synesthesia is not uncommon for those across the spectrum, it is certainly not universal. I also came to understand how the experience could be particularly confusing and disorienting for children. This made me think of all the kids I have known who blankly stare off into space, scream when touched, zone out and rock or use hand stims when music is played, and all those kids who look entirely shut down even though they seem to be looking at something. The statements support the evidence for combined and crossed sensations and a deeply felt version of synesthesia that far exceeds that of typical nerve damage or mixed-message sensory response follows.

I often make unusual sensory connections. For example, sometimes when I hear music, I see all of these colorful moving images in my visual field. As I've gotten older, I realize these visual things are happening only in my mind, but when I was younger, I thought they were actually occurring in the world around me.

I find that my brain often combines sensory sensations. For example, I have described certain smells using texture and can give coherent reasons why I chose those textures. To me, pepper looks prickly because a pepper shaker doesn't give a constant smell. It gives bits of almost pain with less scent in between, like touching a cactus and feeling the sharp spines and the plant underneath.

I have a kind of synesthesia where sometimes the sounds in music seem to form shapes and patterns that I can actually see in my mind. I love my synesthesia; it lets me see things in my mind when I hear music, and this has helped me in my career.

When I was little, my synesthesia was very disorienting and confusing. I saw things that I knew could not possibly be there. I didn't think any other people had the same experience, so I assumed that something was wrong with my brain.

I knew better than to tell people about my synesthesia and the images that occurred when I heard certain things or felt certain textures on my skin, because I knew if I told them they would think I was hallucinating.

As a point I didn't pick up when writing the dissertation, I just now realized that the pattern of synesthesia reported in the study always took the form of a visual sensation. It is in moments like these that I wish I had a dozen more people to ask about synesthesia in autism. If I did, I would ask this question first, "Does your synesthesia always take the form of a visual image?" I am surprised that I missed this before.

Motor Skills and Coordination

With a topic I myself had not considered at the time of the study, although Jean Ayers had clearly articulated this in her work, the statements that follow point to the fact that sensory processing differences also cause one to be uncoordinated. This helped me to see that there is possibly a direct correlation between processing sensory information accurately and responding with "normal" body movements. The ideas below on the topic of coordination also explain why different aspects of difficulty in sensory, gross, and fine motor processing tie into one's ability as a child to socialize.

As I considered these, I immediately thought of all the poor little boys I have known through the years who are truly too clumsy to play with their peers. Significant differences in these areas also explain how sensory-related coordination issues can, when severe, even result in added issues with safety and mobility (recall references to safety in several other categories presented earlier).

All told, I believe we are limited by how well we process and respond to the data of the world outside of ourselves. If we can't process our sensory information, we can't act on it appropriately. My sensory differences have really interfered with my coordination.

My intellectual abilities in some areas were certainly offset by not being able to ride a skateboard, run and dribble a ball, or dance. Anything that would take coordination to do, I didn't do very well. The physical coordination of the other kids was amazing to me. They could ice skate and do all this stuff I couldn't do. I couldn't even run with my hands in my pockets.

From my perspective, I well understood that the physical coordination of others far exceeded my own. The only thing in school I didn't do well at was gym because I am not coordinated at all. I wasn't all that terrific on the playground, either, because I am just not very coordinated. If the girls are all doing double Dutch and you can't even jump a regular jump rope, then you are just kind of out of it.

I feel like when we get to the point where we are so sensory sensitive—touching, sounds, certain tastes, not being able to eat certain foods—then we are just not able to process and that can be a real problem for a variety of reasons. These can even impair our ability to stay safe. If I'm crossing a street and a loud siren goes off, I get disoriented, my knees go wobbly, and I probably am not traveling safely.

Walking on ice is very dangerous for me. I have very slow reaction times and can't correct my movements or catch myself quickly enough to avoid serious injury.

Once, when my sensory system was completely overwhelmed, my body literally just froze. We were on a canoe trip at a boys' camp I was attending, and the other boys had been teasing me and poking fun at me, rocking my boat. Then the boat tipped over. I couldn't move my legs to unlock them from the seat that I was sitting on, even though I was underwater and knew that if I didn't unlock my legs, I would drown. I finally did unlock them, and I escaped from the boat and sort of floated to shore, but for ten or twenty minutes after, I really couldn't walk. I had to just sort of drag my legs to get to me out of there.

Sustainability and Behavior

As I considered the reports of sensory processing difference as a whole category or set, I also found that there was one additional subcategory (or perhaps an overreaching super category) that related to sensory processing and its relationship to sustainable functioning and behavioral meltdowns. As someone who has survived a head injury, I know all too well the ways that sensory processing difference affects stamina and sustainability for day to day functioning. But I had not yet considered how the unpredictable (and sometimes even scary) behaviors that I had observed in those with autism might relate to their significant sensory processing difference. So, with these ideas in mind, I went back to this topic and searched through the transcripts for all statements pertaining to sensory processing differences as these related to functioning and behavior, and this is what I found.

My strategies to deal with sensory issues are always in flux, they have been for fifty years, and they are highly dependent on the amount of energy I have available to process them.

Other people see my degree of deliberation about all these sensory things as ridiculous. But to me, it is necessary, because I can't get in a situation where I am going to spend all my functional energy, then not be able to go to work. It is like if you only had one gallon of gasoline to drive around on all day. Earlier in the day, you'd have more options of where you could drive to. But later in the day, as you've been emptying the tank, your options would narrow considerably.

Sensory processing is a part of my regulation system. I don't think most people understand that. Noisy, crowded, visually distracting workplaces may be cost-effective for the general population, but they are very detrimental to getting any work done for me. I have had to leave work in the past because the environment was so over-stimulating that I was becoming physically ill trying to block it out.

A busy environment, particularly other people talking, is not just distracting, but it's painful and exhausting to experience if I am trying to work. This continual over-stimulation disrupts sleep, impairs my immune system, and is ultimately unsustainable.

My sensory issues assert behaviors that I don't want to come out. I don't know why they are happening, but they are happening. Sometimes when my kids are being rambunctious and loud, I respond. But then I am left feeling like someone else just barked out at them. We have to truly pay attention to that stuff. The "invisible" nature of these issues in ASD leads (NT) observers to assume that those with ASD have a lot more control over their behavior than is really true.

When I was a teenager, we had a flood in part of our house. I remember it clearly because the clean-up completely overloaded me. Although I have never reacted the same way before or since, at one point on the second day I became so frustrated that I literally felt compelled to bang my head on the floor, repeatedly, until it bled. To this day I don't know why I did that, it wasn't me doing it. It certainly scared everyone around me, and I had a headache for about a week, but I really couldn't control it. Afterward, I couldn't really even remember doing it. I knew I must have, though, because people told me I did and I certainly had the bruises to prove it.

My sensory issues assert behaviors that I don't want to come out, that I just can't let come out. We have to pay attention to our state of regulation, or we will be forced to act in a way that we don't want to act. We really have to pay attention to that stuff much more than most people. Sensory differences dramatically affect our performance as we are creatures in a moment.

I truly believe that when we react aggressively or physically, we are often so deeply controlled by our adrenal systems, our fight or flight reactions, that we have very little control over our behavior. I've read something about a topic referred to as "kindling" in the literature, and I think there is something particularly unique about the meltdown behaviors of people with autism in terms of our ability to use something like kindling to release endorphins, calm down, and eventually regain control of our central nervous system.

I have been told that when I am angry, I scream and flap my hands wildly around. Apparently, this scares and upsets people. I'm pretty sure it's true—that I do it I mean—as I doubt people would lie to me about it. But when it happens, I don't have any awareness at all about my behavior. I am so focused on whatever has upset me that I can't come out of that and see myself the way others see me.

I once saw a video of myself that had been recorded by a teacher at my school. I was screaming, flapping my hands, and banging my head against the wall. It was very disorienting to see myself this way. I well remember being upset, and a feeling of heat spreading throughout my entire body, but I had no idea that I had these behaviors or looked this out of control.

As I considered these words, I remembered one of my saddest moments from being a mom with a traumatic brain injury. My husband and I had taken our kids to see a new release of one of the Disney movies, and after exiting the theater, we had made the decision to grab dinner, even though I knew I was far too exhausted to go to a restaurant. In what I remember only as a painfully noisy and chaotic dinner, a magician had been passing out balloons. After the meal we loaded the kids into their car seats, each with a balloon tied to their hand, and rolled slowly out of the parking lot. Just as we moved into the lane, a car raced in front of us and cut us off. This caused my husband to hit the brakes and as if in slow motion, one of the balloons from the back seat came forward and hit me in the head. I completely lost it! Apparently, I was screaming, slapping the air and even slapping at my children. I genuinely felt and reacted as if my life had been threatened. To this day, while I can't easily remember my reaction, I can clearly still recall the looks on my kids' faces. It is still with a great deal of guilt and remorse that I can only be thankful that neither of my children were hurt. Why had I reacted the way I did? What had caused me to lose control to that level? I had never spanked or hit either of my children before.

I spent a lot of time thinking about that night in the years that followed, and ultimately concluded that, like those with ASD, in complete cognitive exhaustion I had reacted entirely from the position of my adrenal system, which in that moment had taken over and responded as if fighting was literally imperative to saving my life. As I read through this section again, editing it for the book, I came to an additional understanding about all of us: our cognitive energy allows us to regulate sensory information processing, emotions, and behavior. Maybe, then, when cognitive energy is depleted through excessive sensory processing for those with ASD, all bets are off in terms of how these individuals will react when startled, injured, or upset.

What this really means to me is that those with autism who are engaged in melt-down behavior might be completely out of cognitive fuel. Could this possibly explain why there seems to be a relationship between those with the most severe sensory disruptions and those with more severe behaviors? Could the topic of sustainability and energy for sensory regulation be a new and improved way to view behavior?

Health and Wellness

Because I had not yet considered the topic of causality in my study, I found it interesting to expand upon the above topic and consider how cognitive exhaustion and heightened stress responses might relate to the topic of sensory difference. When I asked those in the study about this idea, I learned from one of them that one's susceptibility for physical or mental illness directly relates to one's degree of heightened sensory response. Wow! This makes sense. But I had never heard it put so simply or succinctly before.

The idea that heightened sensory response related to physical and mental wellness was especially interesting for me to hear. After my injury, which caused extremely heightened sensory responses, I suffered for almost a decade with a variety of inflammation-based illnesses that caused both physical and mental health challenges. At one point in my recovery, I even had perpetual hives that covered my entire body and lasted for just a few months shy of four years. I also developed severe auto-immune reactions in the form of allergies, even though I had almost no formal allergens. To be fair, I did have one mild allergy (to a specific metal that now lived inside of my spinal column), but it wasn't until I dealt with my stress response and calmed my sensory system down that I became able to tolerate my allergen.

As I combed the research for the combined topics of autism and physical illness, I learned that many with ASD struggle with digestive, hormonal, respiratory, and other physical health challenges. The majority of children with autism also reportedly have significant allergies and food sensitivities. I also learned that within the "lower functioning" forms of autism, a large percentage suffer from seizure disorders. While some of these findings surprised me, what I didn't expect to find is that physical illness has long been correlated to heightened sensory response and overstimulation in autism. This idea is well articulated by the individuals in my study with the following statements.

In one of my jobs I was just so over-stimulated and tired that I kept getting sinus infections until they got so bad that I had to quit.

I had to quit working full time because doing so left me run down to the point that I kept getting sick. I now have to work at a job that is far below my skill level, because I simply can't work full-time and maintain my health.

I am constantly getting sick. Even when I try to take care of myself, with school and work, even part-time, I just can't do it all without making myself physically ill.

I don't believe that I have ever been healthy like other people are healthy. I constantly have to mind what I eat, pay attention to how much I sleep I am getting, and I can't be around toxins at all. Even certain air fresheners or cleaners will make me sick, sometimes for days. Also, my digestive system has never quite worked as well as it should. I either have constipation or I have diarrhea. I am not sure if I have ever in my life had a regular bowel movement.

If I don't pay close attention to my health, I can easily get into a run-down state where I become physically quite ill. On several occasions I have even had to spend a few days in the hospital to recover when I have pushed myself too hard.

It just takes so much energy for me to keep my sensory reactions in check that I exhaust myself quickly and if I am pushed continue, I will get sick.

As I considered this from the position of an educator, the topic made me realize how all of these health-related things might impact learning, performance, and behavior in the classroom. For me, head injury had certainly ruined my health. I had only been able to continue functioning with a lot of supports and accommodations in place and with a shortened work schedule. But kids don't usually get to tell us when they are too tired to go to school or too tired to do their school work. Is it possible that these kids with ASD are really just too exhausted to be physically healthy? Which, then, comes first: their autism or the physical illness that make their autism symptoms worse?

Within my practice, I realized as I thought back, particularly over the last decade, I had seen countless ASD kids that were exhausted to the point of being physically unhealthy. In addition to their learning, cognitive, or behavioral difficulties, many of the kids I had worked with through the years had significant health challenges, and *all* of them complained about being exhausted. This was so prevalent that, without realizing it, I even started using a "how tired are you?" scale in my initial contact with a student. Unknowingly, I had learned that if kids were describing themselves as deeply exhausted, then I would need to schedule much more time with them to get to the bottom of all the problems I would need to address for them to be successful in the classroom. For kids in crisis, I also learned that if a kid was cutting, had suicidal ideation, or significant behavioral meltdowns were on the rise, then a day or two of extremely careful observation at home to relax, sleep, read, and calm their sensory systems down (no screen time allowed) often prevented me from having to hospitalize the child.

As I think about this more, I'm now quite certain that the kids I have seen over the past decade (especially those diagnosed with ASD) are not healthy at all. They don't eat well, they don't get much exercise, and many don't even look healthy. I routinely see dark circles beneath their eyes and most have sallow skin, even in the very young children that I work with. As I think back on this, I remember a model that I was given when I did my cognitive therapy for my head trauma. It explained how energy can be divided into four major sections: (1) cognitive energy, (2) physical energy, (3) social/emotional energy, and (4) the energy that is reserved as fuel for our survival. In the model, my cognitive therapist explained that for those with head trauma, cognitive energy ran short because high amounts of it are needed for compensation. As such, and because energy can't be borrowed from either the physical energy or social/emotional energy "bucket" to continue to function, one must dip into the reserve. The therapist added that "dipping into one's reserve is costly because we must use our adrenal system to do so, and over time this isn't sustainable as it can ultimately lead to physical illness."

As one of the many big *aha* moments I had while working on the study, I wondered if being on the autism spectrum pushes one repeatedly into the use of the adrenals for functioning. Over time, wouldn't this then lead to some of the poor digestion, elimination, and toxicity issues we see in those with ASD? Or maybe it was the other way around; maybe something within autism causes poor digestion, elimination, the build-up of toxicity, etc., and over time, this makes one more cognitively exhausted.

From my own experience, I suspect this whole discussion is just like asking about the chicken or the egg, when in effect both are going on and fueling one another. Irrespective of where this comes from, I came to see that individuals with autism are more susceptible to physical illness and adrenal activation, and this might even explain why there were so many references to safety and sustainability in the transcript.

Sensory Processing and Finding My Voice

While I didn't find much more clarity in the relationship between health and sensory processing for those in the study, one statement stood out to me on the topic of sensory processing for its relationship to energy and being non-vocal. You will see more on this topic in the sections that follow. The statement that first tied sensory processing and speaking together follows.

> As my sensory system continues to change over time, I am finally figuring out how to process sensations better, and as I do that, I can slowly figure out where to find my voice; I am like an astronaut from another galaxy, I have only just begun to make contact.

In this lone statement, I finally started to see how all the above topics about sensory processing difference were starting to fit together. Sensory processing must work effectively and efficiently for everything else to fall into place. A SmartArt image that I used early on to help me formulate how all the sensory pieces fit together, from the perspective of those diagnosed with autism, follows.

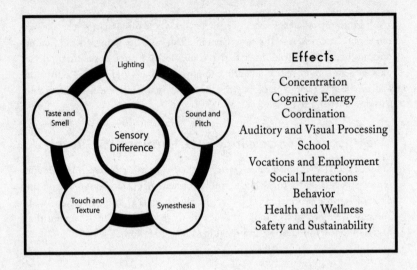

CHAPTER FIVE

What, Then, Is Intelligence?

I knew people thought I wasn't very intelligent because I didn't speak much. But I didn't care. As a kid, I just preferred trees to anything else in the world. In fact, if my parents couldn't find me, they knew to look for me beneath one of the trees in our neighborhood. I knew that the tree had been made, but not made by humans. That was fascinating, it still is. The entire ecosystem of a tree was interesting. Squirrels, birds, colors, forms, it's all so magnificent. Take a walk just after dusk when all the tall trees are silhouetted in the night sky. It's a reminder that there's something out there that is bigger than us. To me, being able to recognize all the beauty that is around us is the purest proof of our intelligence.

With at least two different ways to view the intellect, one from a linear and developmental position of the mind as a machine, and another as a complex mind that has been likened to the cosmos in both its vastness and for our understanding of it, what, then, is intelligence? To put it succinctly, the common and widely accepted formal notion of intelligence is that there are a specific and relatively independent number of brain functions that have the ability to predict cognitive potential and academic achievement and, thereby, dictate occupational success (in other words, how you perform on specific IQ tests dictates how well you will do in school and how successful you will be in your adult life as a working professional). Note that this definition certainly leaves little explanation for those individuals who, in spite of difficulties in school, have turned out to be brilliant professionals (Einstein comes to mind here), or those who did exceptionally well in school but have been unable to secure stable employment as adults.

As the changing times and technologies of the past two decades have moved society into the *information age*, I have certainly wondered if our reliance on the current definition of intelligence makes sense for the twenty-first century in which we live. It seems to me that from the time I went to school until now, schools have not really changed much at all in the ways they teach or even in what they teach. We didn't have computers when I was growing up, and certainly today's children use computers to look up information and conduct basic research (there aren't any encyclopedias lying around anymore). But the curriculum itself is not necessarily that new or different and, as such, it may not be preparing kids for many of today's jobs.

For example, how many kids today are still asked to memorize facts such as "Columbus sailed the ocean blue in 1492?" Isn't that detail, along with the million other unnecessary facts and details that kids still "learn" just a lot of unnecessary, rote information? I have come to realize that, especially for those with ASD, memorized facts and tidbits of detail don't easily generalize into successful or productive adult careers. What, then, do performance scores on all these tests (both academic and intellectual) really measure? If they measure learning, shouldn't that learning, in turn, relate back to success in the adult world? If so, why do so many of today's kids (especially those with ASD) do reasonably well in school, only to become "couch locked" after their formal education is complete? If education doesn't prepare a child to enter the workplace, what is its purpose? It seems to me that, perhaps for the first time in our human history, that what we are teaching doesn't readily apply to adulthood.

The Era of Standardized Performance

While both the *what* and *how* of education hasn't changed much in the last quarter century, within today's version of education, everything has turned toward evidence-based and standards-based practice (for good reason). This gave us the ability to start measuring the effectiveness of our teaching and hold ineffective teachers and schools accountable for ineffective practices. But with this, we have also entered the *era of assessment*. It is estimated that today's kids take tests to show their performance twenty-five to thirty times more frequently than I did when I was a child. That's a lot of testing! While the practice of assessment for various aspects of learning has had benefits, it has also had its drawbacks. I think the biggest of these is felt by children who are neurodiverse.

In this age, where all aspects of education rely heavily on numbers and data, I believe we have taken out of the equation the "gut instincts" about different types of intelligence and performance that gave us some insight into different-minded kids in days past. For children with autism this has been an especially big loss, because with an over-reliance on test scores and a service delivery model designed to bring everyone up to "normal," strengths are frequently overlooked or cancelled out for these kids as their test performance highlights their deficits. It seems to me that many of today's teachers now seem to miss out on the *essence of difference* that their predecessors relied heavily upon for planning and decision-making. Today, the score and not the child drives the education. With these scores using performance numbers as "facts," it is still primarily assumed that over half of all individuals on the autism spectrum have intellectual ability that is in the impaired or disabled range.

Oddly enough, we also can't even turn on the television today without seeing some show about a genius with autism solving some kind of complex problem that no one else has been able to resolve; even our culture recognizes latent genius in autism. I also think most people know intuitively that cognitive and sensory differences negatively affect performance on all tests for those with autism, and that this fact is especially true for the expression of intelligence. So while both educational and mental health systems comfortably accept ASD as a disabling condition, the world at large has positioned autism alongside unusual or even gifted intelligence.

As someone who has tested a lot of kids myself, I know for a fact that some of the visual, spatial, perceptual, memory, and non-linear language strengths that I see in those with ASD are not well captured on any existing test. But, even though performance difficulties in autism are well-supported in both the scientific literature and within the broader society at large, intelligence and academic performance tests are still used to predict academic and vocational outcomes for ASD individuals. This means that these tests drive almost all educational decision-making about placement, services, and supports, and create the very look and nature of what education becomes for these children. Not to belabor the point, but even though we know the tests don't work well for children along the autism spectrum, we still use them because nothing else exists, and our processes for placing a child into specialized educational services still requires the scores.

In my experience of testing thousands of kids, no group of children is less well-represented by the scores they obtain on their IQ tests than those along the autism spectrum. But why is this true? What is it about intelligence tests in particular that makes them so contradictory for individuals with autism?

Spearman's Model of Intelligence

From my perspective, no discussion on either cognitive ability or intelligence is complete without an understanding of how today's ideas about IQ evolved. Put simply (and possibly overly so), during the early years of asking the question "what is intelligence?", Charles Spearman was one of nearly a dozen well-known theorists to propose a construct or idea about what intelligence is. Within the demands of his day, any new constructs required only two things. First, the construct needed to explain intelligence in a way that was acceptable, and secondly, it must be *measurable*.

In those early 1900s discussions, a great deal of intellectual energy world-wide went into thinking about the full range of abilities that cognition could take, and many early theories on intelligence included a wide variety of skills. But there was a darker side, too. With immigrants flooding into the country from abroad, funding for research on the IQ construct was politically motivated to come up with a test that could measure who would and who would not be a benefit to the country. So, because not all the proposed constructs about intelligence could be measured, and some did not take into account how well a person understood and used English, many of these early ideas about intelligence fell to the wayside. This left the remaining researchers in a race to come up with something that would be funded. In those days, the leaders in this race set up testing clinics where they could rapidly design and evaluate performance for a pretty large number of people using "mini intelligence tests."

With a revolutionary twist of fate, Charles Spearman mathematically *invented* factor analysis to process the data coming out of his own assessment clinic, and because Spearman's theory was the only one that could be analyzed mathematically, it became the dominant theory of its time. Essentially, Spearman's construct, which weighed heavily on language, memory, and processing speed abilities, politically met the demands of the day and research moved forward to set the Spearman construct in stone with full funding. Today, Spearman's theory is still primarily the one in use, although Wechsler and others have since added a few additional pieces to the Spearman construct in visual information processing. According to many who have critically reviewed Spearman's work, though, the Spearman theory might not have even been mathematically correct!

When recalculated using modern computing technology (remember, back then the Spearman team had to calculate complex factor analytical models doing all the math by hand), the findings from Spearman's factor analysis of the test data that he collected across what is now referred to as his Holzinger-Swineford data set, suggested "a weak bi-factor model at best." Even though the analytical results were not that conclusive, Spearman claimed them and referred to his intelligence model as "G," or general intelligence. Today, when

Spearman's raw data is reanalyzed using Spearman's factor analysis computed by machine, less than half of the Holzinger-Swineford data is actually accounted for. This means that more than half of the data did not fit the construct that Spearman himself had proposed.

For fun (yes, I am a total nerd), I actually obtained a copy of the data from the Spearman research data set, and for one of my doctoral-level statistics classes, I recalculated the factor analysis for the original Holzinger-Swineford data set for my final project. Along with others in the class, and as confirmed by our professor, I learned that the Spearman model and construct for intelligence would not be an "acceptable explanation for the data" by today's standards. In fact, the Spearman model would be considered a poor explanation for the data analyzed. I suspect that even Spearman knew this, as he attempted to explain intelligence and his unaccounted-for data within the following statement.

> [The model] appears to measure some form of mental energy ... and behaves as if it measured an energy ... there seems to be good reason for changing the concept of energy to that of "power" (which, of course, is energy or work divided by time). In this way, one can talk about mind power in much the same manner as about horse power.

However, even with a poor construct, because Spearman was light years ahead of his time mathematically (and from my perspective, frankly because few people probably even understood what he was talking about), the Spearman model became the model that all future IQ tests used as the basis for their instrument design.

Measuring Intelligence

With that as its history, in spite of questionable assumptions about what IQ tests are still actually measuring today, IQ tests are created and standardized using the Spearman model. This means that the tests are administered to thousands of people until the score data normalizes or can be mapped to a standard bell curve. As such, IQ scores generally have a mean of 100 and a standard deviation of 15, although some tests use a different scale. Thus, for the majority, scores between 85 and 115 are "normal," while scores between 70 and 130 are said to explain intellectual functioning for 98 percent of the population. The terms "intellectually gifted" or "intellectually disabled" are applied to the top and bottom percentiles, respectively.

Within standardized testing practices, while most individuals have scores that are fairly close to one another, it is widely understood that both gifted and intellectually disabled individuals can have highly inconsistent score performance. For them, averaging the various subtests (the individual mini tests used to make up the IQ test) together yields a mean IQ score that simply converges the highs and lows into what results as a single, sometimes meaningless score. This is a problem for any child with individual scores that range outside of what is typical. For example, a child with an average IQ score could actually be intellectually gifted, even though some of their scores are at the bottom of the IQ standard distribution; or the child could be intellectually disabled with a very low averaged IQ score, even though they show strength areas that are much higher and might even be in the gifted range of functioning.

The term twice-exceptionality has emerged to explain a child who is gifted but tests overall into a lower range because of specific deficits. But no term exists for a child with one or two gifted scores that are outside of an otherwise low overall IQ range. In most circles, these children are still most often referred to as intellectually disabled, and their strengths or gifts are referred to as "splinter skills." This is true even when that singularly high score might suggest gifted potential.

Additionally, although IQ scores are believed by most to accurately depict deep and meaningful intellectual abilities for most children, it is widely accepted that a variety of factors can negatively affect the scores. Things like motivation, temperament, language processing deficits, and motor planning issues often cause lower IQ scores. Others have even argued successfully that certain aspects of IQ are culturally dependent.

Intellectual Performance in Autism

Still and most often, the use of a single, averaged IQ score (even though we know it could be comprised of subtest scores that were widely disparate) continues to be the standard for reporting intelligence for those with ASD. With this practice of averaging in place, it is reported in the clinical literature 60 to 75 percent of all individuals on the autism spectrum are intellectually disabled with IQ scores below seventy. This assumption remains unchallenged in the literature, even though newer studies have proposed that even in the most classical and severe forms, autism might be less strongly associated with intellectual disability than researchers have previously believed.

It is also paradoxically assumed that those with ASD cannot easily demonstrate what they know, because there are numerous difficulties in determining IQ in the presence of ASD. Multiple researchers have even found that the use of standardized intelligence tests in ASD are essentially not meaningful at all, based on limitations in verbal communication, problems with social interaction, and associated problems in autism (such as hyper-sensitivity or visual-motor difficulties).

This leaves us with the possibility that there might not be any valid measures to assess global cognitive functioning (or the smaller sets of skills we use to define intelligence) for individuals with autism. But with cognition best defined as "all our mental abilities," what if intelligence that can't be measured does indeed exist, especially for those with ASD? The media would certainly suggest this. In other words, what if Spearman's unaccounted-for data are *hidden* cognitive skills that are more fully developed in those with ASD, but not within today's IQ construct? What if people with autism are smart in ways that we don't recognize or know how to measure? It is clear to me that, in the least, those with autism have some pretty uncanny visual and memory-based skills that I and others like me don't seem to have—even though these individuals often don't test well on standardized memory tests.

Intelligence in Kanner's Autism

In Leo Kanner's 1943 publication *Autistic Disturbances of Affective Contact*, he clearly saw potential and a high correlation between autism and *intellectual giftedness*. This is evident in his clinical report. With the topic of intelligence at the high end of my list when I began my research, I decided to get a copy of Kanner's full clinical report and read it for myself. In it, and not surprisingly, I found that in the original eleven-person case study, Kanner described the "fascinating peculiarities" of eight boys and three girls who presented with an "outstanding, pathognomonic, fundamental disorder" in the "children's inability to relate themselves in the ordinary way to people and situations from the beginning of life" (1943, 242).

As would be expected given what we do understand about autism, Kanner described the following primary problems for the children in his study: (a) preferring to be alone; (b) failure to adopt positive anticipatory postures to being picked up or held; (c) delayed speech or the inability to speak, along with parrot-like responses in speech; (d) fear of loud noises; (e) monotonous and repetitious motions; (f) insistence on sameness; and (g) a lack of normal responding to people.

But within what later came to be referred to as *Kanner's Autism* (which today is still generally viewed as the "lower-functioning" variant of the autism spectrum), what I found most surprising, and essentially lost from main-stream knowledge, was that Kanner clearly indicated "good cognitive potentialities" (1943, 247) for all eleven children. More specifically, Kanner had observed excellent memory skills in *all* the children he studied, and many of his cases showed "good vocabulary." Kanner specifically tied either high potential or giftedness to nine of his eleven cases. I was specifically interested in Kanner's reports of case number one.

In the first case of autism ever reported, Kanner stated "Donald T. could hum and sing many tunes accurately" (217) before his first birthday. Donald also had an unusual memory for faces and apparently could match both the names and faces of all the people in his town to their house numbers when shown a map of the town. He was especially interested in pictures and, by the age of five, could correctly name every image presented to him from the *Compton's Encyclopedia*.

The subsequent ten cases reported similar trends for high potential and, in Kanner's own words, the majority of the cases came from highly educated and professional parents; several worked as university professors. In addition, Frederick, one of the children in the study, even came from "a long line of the genius type" (223) and Richard's family "in both branches, consisted of intelligent, professional people" (225). Additional references to high potential from Kanner included a report of one of the children scoring at least two years above grade level on reading tests, while another with a reported IQ of ninety-four was "without a doubt" (230) much more intelligent than her scores suggested. Kanner's eleven cases even included a boy who "achieved an IQ of 140" (234) when formally tested. In his concluding statements, Kanner added that, remarkably, the parents of the cases all showed high intelligence and the majority of the children's mothers were intelligent and well-educated.

Kanner's initial assumptions and impressions about intelligence in autism were eventually dismissed and, as I see it, the blame for this can be placed directly on the shoulders of Bruno Bettelheim. Based on the belief that the selected group of families who found Kanner were predisposed to be from higher social classes with "intellectual occupations" and many of the mothers of the children worked outside of the home, Bettleheim proposed his "cold refrigerator mother" theory, and after it was debunked, all talk of intelligence in autism was abandoned. This meant that Kanner's suggestion of a very strong link between high intelligence and autism was never explored. More specifically, after Bettelheim, researchers worked hard to conclude that autism can and does occur across all races, nationalities, and social strata, and parenting is not the cause. While this finding was certainly accurate and needed, no additional research on familial intelligence in autism was done for several decades; I personally suspect that after Bettelheim's theory was so completely and soundly debunked, to even bring up the topic of high familial intelligence in autism would have been a deal breaker for one's career. But with nothing to account for high functioning or high intelligence in autism, the door was wide open for Lorna Wing and "Asperger's syndrome" to take up the topic of intelligence in the autism line.

Intellect in Asperger's Syndrome

According to Wing (who reviewed the full clinical files for Hans Asperger), while Asperger's syndrome was initially thought to be similar to autism, it wasn't exactly the same. Wing reported that Asperger described both disabling features and high intelligence from the Asperger cases. Recall that Kanner said this, too! But after reviewing the Asperger cases, Wing felt that there were enough significant differences between the cases of Asperger's and those described by Kanner to explain another condition altogether.

She reported that Asperger described his cases with the following: (a) the condition is not always recognized in infancy, and symptoms might not be seen before the third year of life; (b) speech develops normally, although the content of speech is often abnormal; (c) two-way social interaction is impaired, but not because of the desire to withdraw from social contact—instead, social impairment occurred due to lack of understanding; (d) gross motor movements are clumsy and poorly coordinated; (e) preoccupations and interests exist that generally focus on content subjects, such as a particular topic in science, the history of facts, or characters used in advertising; and (d) the impression of eccentricity. Asperger (according to Wing) added that the condition was genetically transmitted and had the tendency to run in highly intelligent families, adding "the antecedents for generations have been highly intellectual."

Unlike Kanner's cases, though, many of the cases of Asperger's had been formally evaluated for their intelligence on IQ tests of the day; the average IQ score for the Asperger cases was 119. This is especially remarkable when we consider how difficult it is for those with ASD to perform on IQ tests. Using test scores as evidence, Wing then made the case that autism and Asperger's syndrome were distinct and different. With test scores as proof, *The Diagnostic and Statistical Manual for Mental Health Disorders* and the International Billing System both accepted Wing's position until 2015. Asperger's syndrome was diagnosed for children and adults along the autism spectrum who were verbal and seemingly "higher functioning," while non-vocal and more severely impaired individuals were diagnosed with autism.

I would like to reopen the topic of intelligence and Kanner's autism and argue that both Kanner and Asperger felt there was a significant link between high intelligence and the conditions that now make up the autism spectrum. Both reported this in their cases, both clearly articulated gifted familial lineage, and both were impressed by the unique and unusual abilities that existed in their cases in spite of the disabling aspects of the condition.

Savant Syndrome

Going back to the 70s and 80s, another particularly interesting area of research also took up the topic of intelligence in autism; this research focused on the *savant*. Remember that during this time, linking intelligent working moms to autism had become a no-no. As I see it, research on the savant syndrome became an acceptable way to explore strength and latent cognitive abilities in autism. Within dozens of studies conducted over a roughly ten-year period of time, researchers deeply explored children with autism described as "savants." In one of the most prominent of these studies, the "islands of genius amidst profound impairment" concept was born.

Let's be clear, the savant syndrome wasn't new to that generation at all. As far back as the early 1700s, newspaper headings covering the topic of "oddity and genius" highlighted unusual abilities in unusual people. These stories were so popular that some newspapers even had a regular column for them. In fact, one of the first ASD savant stories ever recorded covered the case of Jedediah Buxton, who was described as "a lightning calculator with an extraordinary memory" but had a difficult time taking care of himself. In spite of his significant challenges, Mr. Buxton remained an international sensation, and people had heard of him even years after his death.

The reports and public fascination for the topic of profound ability alongside of significant impairment didn't stop there; hundreds, if not thousands, of stories were written through the years about individuals who struggled with day-to-day things, even though they were geniuses in other areas. I, too, find this fascinating! It is almost as if society wants to believe that those who are smarter can't function like typical people— people like them—in the regular world.

In the heyday of my school, we had a child who was reported to have the highest IQ in the world in attendance. It was later discovered that this child's mother had coached him on the various elements of the IQ test before he was evaluated. The story drew national attention and, as a result, I was interviewed by the *New York Times*. In the article, I made the statement that "the world loves a prodigy, but they love it even more when they can watch a prodigy fall." I think it is within this same sentiment that the savant has captured the attention of so many people throughout history.

Sadly, it is now known that even Hitler was deeply drawn to this topic and actively sought recruitment of individuals with the savant syndrome for research with the hope of figuring out how to capitalize on it. This is probably a good place to mention again that the term Asperger's syndrome, as a diagnostic label, is no longer in use today. The reason for this is an important one, it was discovered several years ago that Asperger personally sent children with his definition of autism (Asperger's syndrome) for "research and disposal" in Nazi-Germany death camps. Thus, at the time this book was in final edit, organizations around the world—including DSM-5 and the international billing code system (ICD-11)—have placed all conditions within autism under a single autism spectrum umbrella and are actively making a concerted effort to eliminate Asperger's name from history.

Today, it is still estimated that at least one in ten individuals on the autism spectrum present with some aspect of a clear savant ability. The most common savant skills include: (a) calendric calculations, (b) photographic vi-sual-memory, (c) graphic and artistic copying abilities, (d) musical abilities for both playing music and recognizing pitch, (e) speed-reading skills, and (f) the efficiency of memorization. According to those who have studied these skills in depth, they cannot be replicated by any population not on the autism spectrum, and "no one researching these curious abilities seriously questions that they can manifest where competence in most other areas of cognitive functioning is seriously impaired" (O'Connor, O'Connor, and Hermelin, 1989, 109). Researchers exploring the savant syndrome concluded that all the unique savant abilities explored in those with autism come from some form of *prodigious memory*.

The Pathology of Superiority

Although certainly not my area of expertise, I have also followed along with interest as the field of neurology has examined some of the unusual strengths that are often seen in those with autism. Within what is now referred to as a *pathology of superiority*, the field of neurology has concluded that compensatory "growth" in one region of the brain can be contrasted against impairment, lack of growth, or injury in another brain region, which causes the majority of cog-nitive differences seen in ASD. In addition to this, just last week I read another article written by J. M. Silela. In it she adds something new to the pathology of superiority by claiming that some of the "copy numbers" within the human genome, which are likened to "volume controls" for our genetic makeup, are different for those with autism. Silela's work, as interpreted by some individuals with autism, suggests that autism is simply a greater magnification for certain, otherwise "normal" brain functions.

But with no shortage of studies about genetic anomalies, physiology, neuro-chemistry, and even visible brain differences for those with autism coming out of the field of neurology and neurobiology, I still have a problem: instead of talking about difference from a position of strength, neurological findings for those with ASD are still almost always described in relationship to impairment. To me, these differences mean that the brain of an individu-al with autism is different. Full stop. Why must difference that is strength-based always look for the associated deficit? Can't we just explore strength for strength's sake? Apparently, that isn't possible when all views are still on

CHAPTER FIVE

"normal" development and fixing what's "broken." In spite of the general assumption that unusually high ability occurs only where severe impairment is also present, gifted and savant abilities are then almost always still referred to as *splinter skills*, even though some of these same exceptional skills and talents would be considered *high abilities* or *giftedness* for individuals with average or above average intellectual functioning.

As such, there seems to me to be a huge difference in how abilities are viewed when the autism label has been applied. In addition to specializing in working with those with autism, I also work with highly gifted and twice-exceptional children; and with this background it is my opinion that in autism, *prodigy* is still viewed as a curiosity and oddity. This results in children without autism, who might have similarly advanced abilities in certain areas, receiving support and assistance to develop their prodigious skill as a gift, while gifts for those with ASD are routinely dismissed and ignored.

Autism in the Gifted

With very few studies to consider the topic of ASD in formally identified gifted children, the field of gifted education also continues to suggest that children can be both gifted and on the autism spectrum. Unfortunately for those with the more severe effects of ASD (speech and motor challenges, for example), proper assessment for the innate cognitive abilities that are present is compromised and these kids never get into gifted programs. Yet, some researchers working in the field of gifted education have concluded that ASD is, in fact, found in "higher-than-would-be-expected rates" in gifted and twice-exceptional populations.

It is additionally interesting to note that multiple studies concur on the topic of giftedness, particularly in the male genetic line for children with autism. At least a dozen studies have found that uncles, grandfathers, and even fathers of children with autism have unusually high rates of representation in the fields of science, technology, engineering, and mathematics (STEM). I know that I personally have seen an unusually high rate of kids with autism who have a gifted sibling.

So again, I ask, what is intelligence? Even more importantly, what is cognition? Do we really know what intelligence looks like in someone who has autism? With no better source to answer these questions than asking those diagnosed, the following chapters provide thoughts about intelligence, cognition, learning styles, and the social and emotional effects of these differences from the ASD perspective.

CHAPTER SIX

Preliminary Thoughts on Cognitive Difference

*I think that there needs to be a distinction between intelligence and wisdom
or discernment. Discernment is often the byproduct of applied intelligence to
the task of independent thinking. I think we often have very sophisticated
levels of discernment.*

As a society, we comfortably accept the idea that we know what intelligence is and we believe we can test for it. Based on standardized test scores, we then make assumptions about underlying cognition. From these assumptions we have created an entire educational system, along with a curriculum to bring children with autism into the mainstream beside their peers. For some kids, this system works, and children emerge reasonably intact with enough information to get them by. For those who think differently, this system is ineffective and sometimes even harmful.

But recall that for much of our human history, formal education was reserved for the wealthy and the scholarly. Across modern times, there have always been accounts of children that didn't do well in school. In generations past, families frequently took their neurodiverse children out of traditional schooling and successfully launched them into adulthood by teaching them to take over a family business, linking them to an apprenticeship for training in a specific field, or by giving them enough practice and skill in the manual labor aspects of farming and ranching so they could support themselves by living off the land.

Views on the Existing System

Within the belief that all children must attend school, today's children have lost other outlets for learning and becoming functional adults. I believe that this has contributed in some part to the increasing number of individuals diagnosed. Even today, no one really assumes that a small number of intelligence-based tests are capable of assessing all cognitive skill. Most of us clearly understand that sensory awareness, attention, creativity, determination, and even some of the nonverbal skills like thinking in pictures are not easily captured within an IQ test. But what if some aspects of cognition that are present for those with ASD are not yet even in our vocabulary about intelligence? Isn't it possible that we, as a collective, have failed to include the skills found within autism in our actual construct for either cognition or intelligence? Here's what those with autism had to say about the existing systems and beliefs.

I would like to start by saying that I think the system is—well, I'm not going to say rigged—but it doesn't work for people like us. All this testing, telling us what we can or can't do ... in thinking back on my childhood, I feel like I was thrown to the wolves. We process everything very differently and we can't always figure out how to process what's going on. When you add blatant hostility and aggression from others, sometimes even teachers, we start to really feel like we don't belong, that we are not very intelligent.

It shouldn't be about what we can't do; it should instead be about each individual's ability, not some comparison to this big yardstick. In today's world, it is attention to a respectful paradigm that we need most. It seems like meeting our needs is just too visionary for the time in which we live. Most people simply don't give a rat's ass about respecting people who are different.

When we are compared to others, we often begin to think about ourselves as not whole people because of all these broken little things we are told don't work for us.

Everyone tries to talk about autism like it is on a linear continuum. I think that is wrong. If you have ever seen a three-dimensional object with x, y, and z, you should think of autism like that—only with a fourth dimension to it, and that fourth dimension in physics is time. In my view of autism, you can have two points in space that are not necessarily connected to each other. But if you fold space, time connects the two points to each other, we now become a whole person.

For us, our broken skills make sense when you think about them in the format of a complex yet still fully functional model. If you are in a three-dimensional system and most of your skill sets are way down here, but you have one or two of these little sets that are way up here, we might think of ourselves as not very functional. But if you bring the points together, like folding a piece of paper, you can line them up, the strengths and deficits, in a way that makes them extremely functional.

Sensory Relationships

From my experience, both professionally and as a survivor of a traumatic brain injury, I have come to believe that cognition in autism is extremely different and simply cannot be compared to cognition outside of autism. I'll add this: I think at least some of these differences in cognition for those with ASD begin within an entirely different system of sensory processing.

I first began to consider the relationships between cognitive and sensory processing differences after my own brain switched from being "neurotypical" to its post-injury state of heightened sensory sensitivity and awareness. As this happened, I also began thinking in three-dimensional pictures for the first time in my life. It wasn't until I found a new way of thinking and sensing that I realized a different aspect of cognition was now present for me. With my background in assessment, it didn't take long to also recognize that no test in the world would be able to measure my newfound differences. It was during this time that I began to explore the significant relationship between differences in processing sensory information and neurodiversity in cognition.

After my accident, my IQ supposedly dropped by almost twenty-five points. Today I understand that my intelligence didn't go anywhere; it just became harder for me to filter out extraneous sensory information, focus on the task at hand, understand the test's directions, and see the right answer instead of the myriad of other possible answers that I could now also justify as partially correct. Additionally, I couldn't perform within the time limits that were given because my thinking was now both slower and more complex.

Now, I believe that I better understand how a different system of sensory processing affects cognition and the demonstration of intelligence. These relationships are also clearly articulated by the individuals who participated in my study. Here's what they had to say.

For neurotypical people (NTs), it all comes together. But for someone with autism, we see everything that goes on around us and we can't sort it. It's like if you take in more than you have the energy to process, then even a simple touch on the hand could feel like a million different things, pleasure, pain, or even a stabbing of pins and needles.

I personally think that people with autism have higher intelligence, or maybe it's a different intelligence, that causes them to take in more information even though they don't know how to process it all. When an individual is unable to filter out extraneous sensory input, it is bound to have a rather permanent effect on how their cognitive abilities develop.

We are very observant of the world around us, but we don't always understand what we are looking at or what we are sensing. That doesn't mean we are not intelligent.

If asked to recall a very specific detail, I often can't separate that specific piece from the sounds, smells, air temperature, etc. that are associated with it. Finding those parts that are specifically visual or auditory is a challenge because everything fits together for me as a whole sensory experience.

I think sometimes our sensory problems can interfere with or hinder speed. I don't think that our sensory differences necessarily determine our intelligence, but I definitely think they are very much a part of the expression of our cognitive abilities. Society defines intelligence as the ability to process information and reason quickly and accurately. I don't have that ability.

Once I understood things better, it really made a big difference. I've seen people over the years come into pop culture with references to autism in movies and television shows, and I think there is a correlation between just how intelligent a person is and what amount of information they can observe and think about.

What is learned is dictated by how you choose or don't choose to process it. I feel like for us, the higher your IQ gets—you see this in savants or those with genius levels of intelligence—it's almost like the more you are able take in and process, the less you are able to put out from that processing.

I don't feel like autism is necessarily lower intelligence, but instead, it might just be a lot more sensory processing.

CHAPTER SIX

Sensory Ties to Cognition

There's a downside to thinking in pictures, though. From my perspective, words became much harder to retrieve and use. In my situation, my word bank (or my actual vocabulary) didn't shrink at all, but I immediately began to stumble and trip over my words with a feeling of being tongue-tied. When I spoke, I often could not retrieve the word I wanted. Sometimes, I even inadvertently substituted the wrong word, and I no longer had the ability to organize my thoughts coherently enough to speak with normal fluency. This was a real problem for me, because I also speak and train teachers and professionals as part of my living.

Early on, I learned that if my brain was just a little tired, and my stress response was quite high, my words were there and sometimes would even come forward better than they ever had before. With this, my best strategy for delivering a good presentation was to go to the session with a broad general idea of what I wanted to say, but without any other formal preparation, and my stress response would do the rest. By working tired, I believe I somehow overrode my new problems with fluency and executive functioning and could then resort back to the deep reservoir of knowledge that I had accumulated prior to my injury. By the way, I could not do this if the topic was something new! In ways I still can't explain, my stress response has allowed me to use reserve energy to function, but this came at the expense of my health. As I literally fell apart both physically and emotionally, the process became very interesting to me, because almost every twice-exceptional child or child with autism that I have ever known seems to dip deep into reserve energies for day-to-day functioning. As this happens, the sensory system activates. With our fight-flight-freeze systems of response, the more cognitively exhausted we become, the more sensory information we are aware of. For me, this worked to help me read my audience and track my presentations.

As another chicken or egg question for those with autism, I wondered: does autism come with heightened sensory response from birth? Does this require more energy to process so that, over time, there is an effect on brain development toward cognitive difference? Or, do those with autism do what I did and dip into their reserves to function cognitively within a set of highly disparate cognitive skills (that presumably came with genetics), and this activates the unique sensory response that seems to accompany ASD? With no clarity for the direction this cycle might take, I dug deeper to explore some of the actual cognitive differences that were present for the individuals in my study.

Sequencing and Cognitive "Glue"

Within what I eventually came to see as a conversion from verbal language to visual sequencing (what I mean by sequencing is the "glue" that binds one's thoughts together), I discovered that one of the most notable cognitive traits for those in my study showed up in the preference to organize thoughts and ideas within a pictorial or sensorial frame of sequencing. As I began my discussions on the topic of cognition and autism, it became pretty clear to me from the beginning that the individuals who had volunteered to help me could not only easily see pictures and recall full-body sensory experiences in their mind, but they often used these to glue their ideas together instead of words or word phrases. As a strong cognitive style, this apparently has an especially noticeable effect on the expression of oral language. Everyone in my study, in spite of their functional language abilities (one woman even fluently spoke eight different languages) described how the way they stored ideas and retrieved them for communication was not necessarily typical. Difficulties for those in my study with untangling their words and using their language are described in the following statements.

I have a theory that I developed over the years from my own experiences of not being able to express myself, either through communication or physically. I think that because I was trying to process so much information (both sensory things and visual ideas in my head) and not understanding how to do that, I struggled with choosing what to keep and what to let go, and that made deciding what is important hard.

I have an extremely large vocabulary, but I can't easily formulate the right language structure to apply to all the images, patterns, and sequences that I see in my mind.

My brain moves a great deal faster than my mouth and I have this whirlwind of information in my head in the form of sights, sounds, smells, etc., so I am constantly stumbling over my words even when I am pretty clear about what I want to say.

There is so much I am trying to filter through this tiny little funnel that is my mouth. I definitely have a great deal of auditory strength, but what's difficult is speaking with a sense of fluency. I mean the thought is already there, it's just that the fluency—the words needed to actually get it out of my mouth—is the problem.

I think for people who are on the spectrum, we often have a higher IQ, but maybe we are not able to convey it as well. Even with me, people make some assumptions because of my mannerisms in communicating that I am not that intelligent. I think the first assumption, until people get to know me or know of me, is that maybe I am not catching on or maybe I am not as smart.

I think it varies from culture to culture, but I think in the U.S., the North American context for sure, the ability to speak clearly, to speak at length without pause, is supposedly a sign of someone who is very bright. So, when you have problems getting the words out, the assumption is that it is because of a lack of mental ability and not some other reason.

You know, the position I always take as an advocate is that there is such enormous potential within each one of us, and yet, how do you define what intelligence is? Is it what you are taking in, how your brain works, or is it how you communicate or articulate that knowledge to the rest of the world?

Unfortunately, in most settings, intelligence is assumed based on how easily or efficiently one can or cannot communicate.

The ability to see a problem, but not express it convincingly in words, is deeply frustrating.

I am a visual thinker. But when I see things, I often don't know words for the things I can see. It seems that our problems with fluency and verbal communication skills are often our greatest setback.

I may always be more non-vocal than others, but I am surprisingly quite verbal in my head. Using one's voice is a particularly energy-consuming task. Perhaps it is why few animals on earth have any degree of sophistication in their communication systems.

Knowing that we are, in general, more visual in our thinking, why are we not tapping into communicating through visual languages for some of these nonverbal children?

I learned about visual sequencing a number of years ago. It began when one of the kids I was working with tried to explain his thinking to me by asking me, "What is a fire truck, what is the first thing that comes to mind when I say the word fire truck?" I replied by stating, "Well, it's a vehicle that puts out fires." He then explained to me that his brain just saw pictures: a red truck, men in yellow suits, various gears and hoses on a control panel, and even a dalmatian hanging off the back of a moving fire truck. In that moment, I learned that there are at least two ways to glue ideas together. The first, like branches on a tree, takes a word and expands it into its correct definition. But for those who think in pictures, a bunch of different pictures (in my mind I see them as thought bubbles) bounce around in no particular order. As such, it usually takes quite some time for a visual sequencer to get their fire truck—or rather, the picture that is in their mind of a fire truck—to an actual fire. In fact, as I have repeated this question for my own clients, I have learned that some never mention anything at all about putting out a fire. As I have understood this better, I have added my own question. For someone who seems visual I ask, "Is the picture of your fire truck flat like a photograph, or can you easily see it from many different orientations in your mind?" Having conducted this test now hundreds of times, I have learned that flat-picture sequencers can eventually find their words, although they are much slower than verbal sequencers and still start with a picture first. But a truly spatial thinker struggles to even describe a fire truck, because the vast array of possible three-dimensional and spatial images they have tied to the concept of "firetruck" becomes nearly impossible to quickly capture, prioritize, and put into words. I will add that very intelligent children with good language-processing skills in other areas (such as abstract verbal reasoning) might learn to predict the expected answer (which most people assume to be the verbal answer), even though that is not their original or first answer. For me, pictures were still mostly flat, but I never lost my ability to sequence in words. Within these nuanced yet really big differences, I began to consider the impact that visual and sensory sequencing had in the traditional learning environment.

Views on Education

In the classroom, the skills of listening, reading, writing, and communicating orally have always been paramount. Even now, with all the complex visual technologies and information systems we use in our day-to-day lives, most schools are still heavily indoctrinated with teaching through words and verbal sequencing. This means that if you don't sit still and learn by either reading what has been placed in front of you or listening and understanding what the teacher has to say, then you can't quickly organize and articulate a concise verbal response in words or on paper. Moreover, if sequencing impairs your ability to efficiently get your knowledge out into written or spoken words, you can't efficiently demonstrate your learning in school, and this causes you to appear less intelligent overall.

But believe it or not, there are many other ways to learn and demonstrate learning, and there are many vocations that don't rely heavily on speaking or writing. My daughter is an artist, for example. While she certainly must listen and respond to her client's needs, once she has a visual image in her head, very little language-based thought or sequencing is needed to complete a project. I think that for lots of kids with ASD today, the actual educational system and even the core definition of learning is particularly ineffective in helping them reach and excel in avenues for learning that might be more aligned with their strengths. This is true even though the modern workplace offers a wide variety of hands-on and experiential learning, which demands strong visual logic and sequencing and expects visual or physical products. Yet schools still teach through listening, reading, speaking, and writing. In my view, this is not the best way to prepare ASD individuals for the workplace. Insights about education from those with autism who volunteered for my research follow.

I often think that it is a particularly autistic solution to the problem of a difficult environment for those of us with ASD to change the environment, rather than to change the person, but others don't see that as necessary. I think that most people are just too callous and too mean to care about people like us.

You, as an educator, are probably looking at me on the autism spectrum within the lens of the neurotypical world, which expects us all to be in the center of some imaginary axis. We are on a different axis altogether, especially as it relates to how we think and learn.

In addition to my strong visual memory, I could also remember everything the teacher said. It is why I did so well in her class. Everything she said was on the test. I can recall verbal facts easily; I'm especially good with trivia. My visual memory isn't as strong, especially for short-term memories, but my visual memory is much better when it is tied to something that interests me. Even though I did well in school, school didn't necessarily prepare me for my adult life.

With tremendous visual and verbal memory and the ability to access it, when I was young, it just came forward so quickly and that passed for intelligence. The reason I won the spelling bee was that the spelling bee was limited to a few thousand words and I just memorized every single one of them.

It is like the higher the IQ gets, the more different your thinking becomes, and the more assistance you need to translate what you are taking into what you can put out, but we don't always get that help in the classroom because everything around us is just moving so fast.

I believe, especially when we are children, that we seem to be thinking slower because we are taking into account more specific variables and more information in our thinking. But no one really helps us with that.

When I took a test, it wasn't necessarily that I understood the subject matter, I might have, but the advantage I had was that I could remember everything the teacher said. All I had to do was write it down. Because I had this tremendous verbal memory, I got tagged as being particularly intelligent. When I got out of school, I was still missing important conceptual information that was beyond the reach of my verbal memory.

Many autistic people are gifted in a technical sense and are lucky enough to establish careers in professions such as coding or engineering, which is presumably tied to their strong visual learning style. I am also visual in some ways but also very gifted in the humanities and with learning foreign languages, so I did well in school. But even with that traditional school background, I, and others like me, have found it difficult to apply these language skills to the workplace, since these types of fields often also involve a high level of social interaction ability, which we don't possess.

Injury in Autism

As discussions on the topic of education evolved for those in this study, almost everyone I spoke with eventually came around to talking about children who are more severely impaired. Invariably, these conversations progressed into a view that I learned those within the autism community share: it is apparently widely believed by those with autism that some individuals with autism are "injured."

This concept was new to me, although my own background specifically includes work with very "low-functioning" individuals. In fact, my first paid position after my initial behavior training in autism involved work in a group home specifically opened to house the last six (and most severely affected by autism) patients as they transferred out of the Utah State Hospital system.

The phrases and statements that came through by those diagnosed supported a premise that autism was first and foremost a neurodiverse learning style, passed down genetically through families. But due to heightened sensitivity that accompanies the cognitive difference in autism, this learning style is also one that is particularly susceptible to injury from things like pesticides, hormones in food, chemicals in the air or water, and the like. As it was proposed by various individuals in the study, here's what they had to say.

Though I can find many examples of Asperger traits in my family tree going back for many generations, the incidence of "low-functioning" autism is unprecedented for us prior to my children's generation. This leads me to consider the possibility that this generation of Asperger children might be injured "Aspies," with that injury localized to their corridors of interacting with the world. Two of my own children are so "damaged" by their autism that they can hardly be considered intelligent.

In spite of a gifted genetic lineage, I feel two of my sons are most likely intellectually disabled, although I can never be certain what was innate or what has been the result of damage—they both have had thousands of seizures.

If a kid doesn't have a vehicle to communicate, where would he acquire information and how would he articulate his intelligence? How would you know his intelligence? I think these kids are autistic in how they think, they just have some aspect of processing that has been damaged.

Every kid with autism I have ever run into seems to be plenty intelligent to me, and in my work, that is a lot of kids! They just can't figure out their world because something has damaged their filtering mechanism. I have been around some kids that are very "low functioning" or non-verbal. But I think even for them, it is just more a question of accessing it or putting them in an environment where they are able to express it.

My own children are more severely autistic and essentially nonverbal. In their cases, they are very intelligent in similar ways to others in our family, but it seems like they don't have a reliable input/output corridor to draw upon. I believe that something has damaged their brain to cause this.

I don't know how this works in practice, but in theory, I believe that even kids who are very severely autistic could be taught to understand what is going on around them. We have a very visual and sensorial way of accessing the world. Once I was able to learn to process the world around me, I went from being "lower" to "high functioning." I feel like you should approach autism from the standpoint that all these kids are intelligent, but some of them are in pain or they are sick, and they just can't figure out their sensory systems.

I think the idea of classifying kids as "low-functioning" or nonverbal should be re-thought entirely. Too many of these kids have proven themselves to be very verbal and highly intelligent once their health allows them to learn a method of communication that doesn't require their vocal cords.

I don't believe that we all need to be cured or even have our differences prevented, but whatever environmental things are injuring our children to these more severe levels does need to be figured out and prevented if at all possible.

We do need to understand that, for those of us who are or have been very low-verbal or non-vocal, we have actually suffered some damage within our sensory and language processing systems. For this reason, I think we must first teach kids with ASD how to manage sensory inputs. Then, I believe their communication and functioning will eventually improve.

I believe that I still can't speak because the part of my brain that allows me to direct my energy toward speaking has been damaged in some way. I feel fairly certain that I have sustained some injury from environmental or chemical toxins.

Learning Styles in ASD

As we read through the statements above on "injury in autism," I'm sure you noticed, as I did, two separate themes: injury and the topic of genetic or familial learning style. With some indication for the possibility of "visual or sensorial sequencing and organization style," but really nothing more than the same statements you have read to this point, I began to ask the individuals in my study about their thoughts on genetic differences, learning styles, and deeper cognitive differences.

At first, I got very little from my discussions and on more than one occasion I was given this quote, "If you have seen one person with autism, then you have seen one person with autism." But as the conversations expanded, this statement didn't prepare me at all for what I was about to hear next; not only are there at least two (and probably three) very different learning styles in autism, but these style differences are significantly more pronounced and extreme for individuals with autism than they are for those who are neurotypical. The statements that introduced and clarified these initial points about learning style difference in autism follow.

I guess I still don't really know how different my thinking processes are. I know that we tend to be visual thinkers, but some of us, like me, do not seem to think very visually in some ways at all. I believe that because for many of us, our thoughts occur in such rich, sensory detail, our vision is just such a small and singular component of our entire experience.

There appears to be remarkable difference between us in our visual skills versus our verbal skills. There are those of us that are verbal facts people and there are those that are visual and sensory information processors.

That difference seems to be fairly entrenched within us, even when we are young and to a much greater degree than is seen in those without autism.

For some reason, one that nobody seems to understand, there are those of us who just cannot do math. I mean, we really can't do math! It isn't just challenging or hard for us, we can't compute. In my way of thinking, math can be broken down into two parts: basic number manipulation (arithmetic) and understanding math concepts (which I do well because it is quite visual). It is that conceptual understanding that allows some of us to be able to us to apply math concepts to solve real-world problems, even though arithmetic is still really hard.

It seems that for those of us on the spectrum, we are either math-phobic or language-phobic. I have noticed that we either can't spell and write, and I mean this very literally, or we can't do math.

We can either write and compute basic arithmetic or we can produce in mathematics and physics. Arithmetic isn't math.

Some of us remember everything that was said (verbal facts people) and then there are those like me that remember sights, smells, sounds, and melodies (this participant is blind). I believe we process very differently, and use either a verbal or a visual system, based entirely on how much sensory information we are working with.

I am not so sure that there is that much of a core difference between us internally or in our learning styles, although I think the main difference is in having a viable corridor for processing and communicating; I think that whichever one is stronger, the visual or the verbal will be utilized and developed to a very different degree.

Coexisting Learning Disabilities

This opened up another line of discussion for one of the participants who is also severely dyslexic (unable to read). His words have since become my best description, to date, to explain reading disabilities in a deeply visual thinker. The participant who shared the following information also added that he can read in French or other foreign languages much easier than he can read in English.

This seemed like a singular anomaly until I specifically asked others, who also reported some lessor difficulties with reading; I then learned that two other people (three total in this group of seventeen) preferred to read certain things in French or another foreign language over reading in English, even though English was the first and primary language for all of the research participants. Perhaps somebody who understands the structure of the English language as it compares to other language systems can explain this to me, but the supporting statements about reading, reading disabilities, and challenges with reading in English, follow.

I was very dyslexic in addition to having autism. I couldn't read until I was about eleven years old, although I know others with autism who are precocious readers when they're very young. I think that I am just so overly visual that I can't pin letters or shapes to a fixed position.

When I read, in my mind I can see every letter and every letter combination in every word, and sometimes every word combination in every sentence, all at the same time. This makes reading rather challenging for me.

In terms of learning languages, I did okay, as I could memorize a huge amount of vocabulary—but reading and grammar were much more difficult. There were so many exceptions to the rules that it seemed easier to map French, German, or Latin onto English, which I spoke intuitively, for reading and writing.

When I struggle to read something in English, I often get a copy and read it in French. Even though English is my native language, I can sometimes read better in a foreign language.

Views on Classical Intelligence in Autism

Because the research study behind this book drew participants who were connected to me through the U.S. Autism and Asperger Association or had come to me through my private practice, the people that ended up contributing to this work were all reasonably "high-functioning." Many had been diagnosed with Asperger's syndrome, several had become professional trainers in the field of autism, and certainly all were considered "bright" by today's standards. But when I specifically asked about the topic of intelligence and explored whether the individuals in the study had ever taken an IQ test or felt intelligent, I received some interesting insights and challenging views. In particular, the construct of intelligence as it had related to adult functioning for those with ASD was especially controversial for this group. Here's what they had to say about the topic of intelligence within autism.

I have always been told that I am a very good abstract problem solver. This feels accurate, although I'm not necessarily intelligent in traditional ways.

I've been told I'm incredibly smart. Some days that seems accurate; other days I'm barely functional and I wonder if Mensa accidentally mixed up my scores with those of someone else.

My IQ test was pretty much inconclusive with too many highs and lows to derive a meaningful IQ score, although I've been told I'm highly intelligent.

I don't necessarily consider myself that intelligent but the end result, when I took the test, ended up being very surprising. I ranked in the upper 2 percent of genius. The score didn't feel true to who I am, or to my academic experience, or to who I perceived myself to be, because I have to work so hard to get there in ways others don't.

I suppose I gave the impression of being intelligent, but I've always felt anxious about learning that for which I have little interest. I disagree with some knowledgeable people who say I am more intelligent.

I've always done well playing Trivial Pursuit and *Jeopardy*. I'm very interested in the current election campaign. So, I would say I feel most intelligent in the areas of general knowledge, but I'm not sure how helpful that is in other ways.

I've actually been told throughout my life that I'm intelligent, gifted even, by teachers, college professors, work supervisors, my best friend, and my current therapists. I'm not really sure that is true or that their definitions of intelligence even really apply to me.

CHAPTER SIX

My mother was told by one of my high school teachers that I had a very high IQ, although I don't recall if this opinion was reached as a result of an actual IQ test or standardized testing. I did well on tests, but then other things were just so challenging that I am not sure the tests predicted what they were supposed to.

With my tremendous recall and the ability to access information, especially when I was young, it all just came forward so quickly and that passed for intelligence, but I am not sure that was intelligence. I never took an IQ test, but I don't think I am nearly as smart as people think I am.

I was classified with Asperger's, so I really can't discuss the entire spectrum. But I think, at least for people with Asperger's, there seems to be a tendency to sort of have an IQ that is higher on the scale than average. But I'm not sure that can really be compared to those who are NT, and we can't always test to that level.

People with Asperger's syndrome are often portrayed or considered to be more intelligent than normal because they can demonstrate high levels of competence within narrow skillsets. This can suggest that the gaps in their competence are deliberate. They aren't.

The popular understanding of different types of intelligence (IQ, EQ, etc.) helps in some respects, but with a big caveat. I think what we know can be very specific to only one or two areas. But perhaps having a high IQ can help us to compensate for some of that rigidity?

I am often asked, "How does someone who is so intelligent do such stupid things?" I think many of us on the spectrum are almost just too intelligent for our own good.

I feel that the type and level of intelligence one has and how it's applied can vary very widely throughout the autism spectrum. There are just so many different types of intelligence, whether it's emotional, social, intellectual, memory, planning, or problem-solving. But every person with autism is different. Therefore, it's a bit difficult to generalize about intelligence in ASD.

Some nonverbal people are actually gifted with a genius-level ability in areas such as mathematics or music, but then lack the ability to perform the mundane tasks associated with independent living. I don't believe that NTs are necessarily more intelligent than the mute musician or mathematician who needs help with self-care, or than the well-educated Aspies stuck in menial jobs. But they might feel like they are, because they seem to be able to do more things.

I've limited my answer to how different types of intelligence among people with ASD will or will not help them thrive in the workplace and, therefore, enable them to live independently. In that narrow definition, I am afraid we are not very intelligent.

I have met so many incredibly brilliant people who have autism—and when I say brilliant, I mean some very specific things, like they are dead-on insightful about certain areas, but then can also be totally clueless about others.

I believe that "higher-functioning" people with ASD are more gifted intellectually than the average neurotypical; we must be highly intelligent to be able to compensate for so many things. However, the ability of the ASD person to adapt to a neurotypical world will very often determine how well he or she can put those gifts to use. I'm afraid we often don't appear very intelligent.

One's ability to adapt should be yet another measure of intelligence. You can have tremendous skills, all sorts of fragmented abilities, but if you can't piece those fragments together, does that limit your intelligence?

Even though I have my doctorate in education, the highest IQ score I ever got in formal testing was right around eighty. I doubt my IQ is actually that low! When I was young, my parents were told that I should be institutionalized because my IQ was so low. But now I travel and lecture all over the world, so it must not have been that low after all.

Taking what I had learned from these words, I began to understand that, at least for those with autism, IQ scores and even the underlying construct of intelligence might not be particularly accurate. While the scores might still measure certain things at the exclusion of other things, they might also overestimate potential in certain areas while missing other areas of deficit. Also, even when the scores are well above average or even in the gifted range of performance, they don't necessarily appear to do what IQ scores are actually supposed to do, which is predict academic or vocational success for individuals with autism.

As I explored this topic further, I learned that many adult individuals with autism believe within today's school system (with heavy reliance on test scores and standard performance), kids with autism have been "dumbed down" even more than they were in years past. I also learned that for those with children who don't have the numbers to prove it, claims about the possibility of higher potential go largely ignored.

This reminded me that in my private practice over the last decade, I have attended at least twenty-five special education meetings in which parents of children with autism had specifically called on me for assistance. In almost all of these, part of my job was to relay the parents' belief that their child was actually much higher in potential than had been reflected within the school's testing. In two of these cases, the fathers of the children being discussed were also most likely on the autism spectrum, as they had been particularly late to bloom although they now held down good professional jobs.

With what seemed like an easy task to me after meeting the children, I quickly learned how prevalent assumptions really are within the school system. In almost every case, I found that teachers doggedly used test scores to show why the child needed to continue to work on basic vocational or even pre-academic skills, even when the child had been able to produce grade-level work when working with an aide, a tutor, or when working with the assistance of a parent in a quieter, after-school home environment.

In more than one instance, even though the parent or teacher working outside of school had produced volumes of student work, the school had even accused the parent or tutor/teacher of lying or making up the child's capabilities because, according to them, the student had never done that level of work in the classroom.

Having worked in the classroom, I realize how challenging it is for teachers to accept that a child is really functioning three, four, or even five grade levels higher when in school versus when one-on-one and/or outside of the school setting. But in autism, I know this trend is common. These kids look smarter and do better when not in school. So, how should educators design curriculum and programs? If they assume the child to be intellectually capable at the parent-reported level, even though he or she can't ever perform to that level in school or outside of a one-on-one setting, then they can't track progress. Which is, by the way, required. But if the child really can perform higher in some settings, shouldn't they be challenged and have their strengths developed? While these questions don't have easy answers, perhaps the answer lies in digging deeper to gain a more complete understanding about cognitive difference in autism.

Statements from this chapter suggest that individuals with autism think differently and have extreme differences within their sensory processing systems. These differences affect sequencing (the glue that ties our thoughts together), oral language, and possibly even increase susceptibility to injury. Furthermore, extremes in learning style appear to be much more pronounced for those with autism than for those in the general population.

But what, then, is at the heart of sensory and cognitive difference for those with ASD? What really makes someone with autism tick? Up to this point in my study, I was still thinking about thinking within my professional training. I had not yet driven away from my own developmental world views, and I was trying to make everything I discovered fit into my own existing beliefs. But what came next took me straight off the cliff. As I dug deeper into cognitive difference in autism, I learned that something very different about memory and focus drives cognition and how it has evolved for those with autism. Hold on, because you, too, are about to enter the mind of true neurodiversity.

CHAPTER SEVEN

Discovering Neurodiversity

I can say based on my own experience with autism and having taught many other people on the spectrum that our ability to acquire certain information, retain it, then see or sense unique patterns is pretty unusual and sometimes even pretty bizarre. I mean that in a very positive way.

With approximately 100 billion brain cells simultaneously connecting to tens of thousands of other cells, it is clear to me that human cognition is, by far, much too complex for us to even scratch the surface on understanding. Yet you will recall that early behaviorists (often using animals as subjects), believed pretty much anything could be trained or taught, and cognitive performance could be observed, reinforced, and measured.

The Cognitive-Learning Theorists

Even back then, not everyone agreed, as was discussed in the chapter on sensory processing theory. Early neuropsychologists such as Jean Ayers thought differently about cognition and performance, reminding us that there is nothing linear or observable about the process of thinking. The behaviorists were also criticized by another group of researchers and scientists. Referring to themselves as cognitive-learning theorists, this group also claimed that behaviorism had too narrow of a view on cognition. Their work shifted to consider topics in learning that were much more complex and deeply seated than either Watson or Skinner had suggested would be possible.

Drawing heavily from the field of computer science, the cognitive-learning theorists quickly came to the assumption that the brain was like a computer. This led them to propose numerous parallels between computer models and the human brain. Some of the primary topics researched by the cognitive-learning theorists included verbal learning, the use of visual imagery in learning, learning through active discovery, generative learning (how learners construct meaning from their own base of previous knowledge), and language mnemonics (the way that someone remembers, organizes, and retrieves their language).

The work and research of the cognitive-learning theorists gave way to some truly interesting ideas about dual-processing (thinking or problem-solving across more than one task at once), *top-down versus bottom-up* thinking

(thinking from a part to the whole or from the whole to its parts), and other, more complex information-processing tasks such as thinking about one's own thinking. The field also gave us research on learning in the absence of formal instruction, new ideas about attention, and even a deeper understanding of the role of self-determinism in learning. These added some much-needed complexity to worldviews on cognition, and they shifted interventions (slightly) away from simple behavior training. In the study of autism, this specifically opened the door to explore how relationships influenced learning, and programs like floor-time, joint-attention, and social skills programs that reinforced socialization for socializations' sake emerged.

Like behaviorism, though, the cognitive-learning theorists still surmised that cognition came from the "brain as an object" and was, therefore, capable of being understood through the dissection and reduction of its processes. In this worldview, even within the expanded views of the cognitive-learning theorists, it was also still assumed that the workings of the mind could be reduced and analyzed through examination of its hemisphere lobes, structures, and systems of processing.

Very little has changed in this field since its inception, although in recent years, within the cognitive-learning tradition, research has further explored the role of experience in learning. Secondarily, this field has also opened the door to some fun and exciting developments in artificial intelligence; but in my opinion, even the AI world is still a long way off from understanding and replicating anything close to normal human intelligence. This still leaves our understanding worlds away from capturing the essential differences in cognition that I believe are present in autism.

In the past decade, the behaviorists and cognitive-learning traditions have finally joined up with the cognitive neurosciences, and this had resulted in the production of some high-level information-processing simulations. Advanced medical equipment that makes certain aspects of information processing more observable and replicable has also been invented. But nearly all of what is still understood about cognition still comes out of either the behavioral or the cognitive-learning tradition and, as such, cognition is still primarily thought about as either an experimental or a systems-based process that relates primarily to the tasks of language-based information processing, memorization and recall, and efficient visual-motor production. Even with all of these advances, Nichols and Newsome stated my belief about our understanding of cognition when they said this: "The deepest mysteries facing the natural sciences today concern the higher functions of the central nervous system ... understanding how the brain gives rise to mental experience looms as one of the central challenges for science in the new millennium" (1999, c35).

Introduction to Thinking Differently

While my head injury shaped my own thinking for over a decade, another equally profound shift came to me in a single *aha* moment. I, along with two other advisory board members, was sitting behind the stage at a national autism conference while the keynote speaker, Dr. Temple Grandin (a now-famous adult with autism) made an off-hand comment. In it she stated, "NASA and MIT are, in all likelihood, sheltered workplaces for individuals with autism." While at first I thought she made the comment as a joke, as I thought about this further, I came to realize that Dr. Grandin was most definitely onto something. As proposed by both Kanner and Asperger, there is apparently some relationship between high cognitive ability, especially in STEM fields, and the condition of autism.

As Grandin continued to discuss differences in cognition alongside of sensory processing differences for those with ASD, I arrived at my own personal conclusion: the various ways that cognitive and sensory processing differences combine for those with ASD (and maybe even as they had done for me after my TBI) might, in fact, explain why so many of my clients had found vocational success, even though their IQ scores and academic achievement had predicted otherwise. Many of the people with autism that I knew were somehow using what appeared to be unmeasured cognitive skills (skills largely not recognized within our framework about intelligence, learning, and even education), and in ways no one clearly understood, were finding success.

Emerging Cognitive Differences

Though this topic held no shortage of data from the individuals helping me with the study, because my own thinking was still quite neurotypical in some ways (particularly in my skills of verbal organization and sequencing), the logical placement of the ideas that followed were really difficult for me to figure out. I found myself going back and forth between (a) the idea that sensory processing differences contribute to an already different style of cognition and include such things as memory and focus; or (b) the notion that because sensory processing was significantly different for those with ASD, a different form of memory, focus, and ultimately cognition has evolved. I finally decided that the problem could not, in fact, be resolved within a linear dialogue, because these seemingly opposite positions were both cyclical and recursive. I therefore made the decision to place the sensory differences first in both this book and in the dissertation, even though I also firmly came to believe that innate cognitive differences in ASD are also present in early childhood.

Beginning with the sensory differences described in previous chapters for those with autism, I learned that sensory processing includes more details, is broad, and might even be more sophisticated. This is compounded in autism by an inability to filter (or narrow down) certain sensory channels. Because filtering is difficult, it requires more cognitive work and energy. In turn, this results in sensory differences that cause those with autism to be either highly sensitive to things like lights or sounds, or to tune out sensory information completely. These differences set the stage for an altered cognitive experience.

With this as my starting place, I concluded that for those with autism, some aspect of "normal" filtering of the sensory world is combined with the problem of having more sensory information to filter in the first place. For those who don't tune out entirely, sensory filtering, fatigue, and dysregulation is the result. Over time, this becomes unsustainable. In other words, people with autism can either try to attend to everything, or they can block out everything and hyper-focus. But the task of attending to one thing while ignoring and blocking out another is exhausting, unless one can hyper-focus and ignore everything else. This logically led me to ask, "What, then, dictates your focus?"

Focus

In this area, with my clinical background in assessment and diagnosis (which includes understanding and diagnosing attention deficit disorders), I approached the topic and the discussions with my research participants with more than a bit of a preconceived notion about attention and focus. In my mind, the alignment between autism and attention-deficit disorder was a close one. Recall that within the review of the various cognitive-behavior models that have attempted to explain autism, one of them specifically addressed attention and focus: the theory of executive functioning.

Expecting to see some aspect of attention deficit, it didn't take me long to recognize that within the words of my participants, focus and attention were something very different than what normal or standard views about "attention deficit" might suggest. Most notable was the idea that people with autism are able to focus on some small aspect of a task to a degree that is unusually uncommon, even though their focus is generally associated with focusing on one thing at a time and being unable to switch tasks.

This topic led into the concept of hyper-focusing, and subsequently this gave me some useful insight into the ways that those with ASD might be able to see systems or detect patterns that most neurotypical people miss. This section concludes with what I found to be another unique insight, one that ties observation of the physical world to an understanding of the metaphysical for many people with autism. Two statements that I think really opened the door on the topic of focus follow.

I think for us there are notable differences in how we focus, but it is certainly not an inability to focus. Our attention can be hyper-focused to a degree that most NTs will never reach, this is the basics of autism 101.

I have a marked ability to focus on one thing. I believe that most people with ASD have a superior ability to focus their concentration on a very particular task for long periods of time, to the exclusion of all else.

We tend to be able to focus on and notice design and complexity embedded within what might seem to others as chaos. That alone can be fascinating. But when that design has metaphysical ramifications, it becomes even more compelling.

Multi-Tasking

I was beginning to understand, despite their "marked ability" to focus on one thing, the group was also reporting significant challenges with multi-tasking. Why? If individuals with autism can focus, even hyper-focus, why can't they switch focus and multi-task? The only participant in the group who did not feel she had significant issues with multi-tasking went on to describe how her secretary prepares her in advance, step-by-step, for all her daily activities. This included things like where she would sit, who would likely be sitting next to her, what her schedule would be, and even when she should take a bathroom break. This person also reported that she was unable to clean her house or cook meals for herself and had been forced to hire a housekeeper and assistant to manage things at home, as these tasks were "too boring and tedious" for her to execute.

For the other volunteers, many examples of multi-tasking difficulty were identified. The final comments in this section introduce us to an interesting world-view about multi-tasking, and one of the volunteers even offered a theory that explains why multi-tasking, even within capable focusing ability, might be so problematic for the majority of those on the spectrum. The comments that supported these ideas follow.

I believe that others see executive functioning as a shortcoming for us Aspies; it isn't. I focus, and I recall information just fine, I just can't multi-task. I don't multi-task well because I am specifically focusing on one thing. I can focus on one thing better than most people.

I think it has a lot to do with our marked ability to focus on one thing and marked inability to multi-task. Everything about me that you could say is a downside, there is also a way to see it as an upside.

I can't multi-task, but I can "single-task" better than anyone I know. The way we see it is determined by how the numbers break down. If 99 percent of the population were like me, then we would not live in a multi-tasking world, we would live in a one-tasking world and it would be the people who were bad at one-tasking who would have a syndrome.

Over the years I have developed the concepts of dynamic and static imagination. Essentially, anything which requires someone to think "what if . . ." during a process requires dynamic imagination and is not suited to people with autism. But anything which can be pondered offline and built up gradually into a larger structure requires static imagination. Thus, a person with autism could produce impressive works of musical composition or imaginative drawings if left alone but fail completely to perform in real-time or explain these to someone else. Perhaps what I am simply over-elaborating is our very, very poor ability to multi-task!

Focus and Sensory Processing

While this next theme was something I intuitively related to from my own experiences, I had never specifically considered how significant the relationship is between focus and sensory processing difference. The statements that follow make it clear how these fit together.

> Others have the tendency to believe that we have a diminished capacity to allocate our attentional resources and, for this reason alone, we can't process sensory information. But anyone with ANY autism experience can refute that. I do well to focus on one thing. However, if the one thing that is vying for my attention is a sensory thing, say an uncomfortable bump in my sock, I have to get rid of it. If I can't stand to have socks and shoes on; I have to take them off or I am not going to be able to concentrate. My hyper-focusing is not limited to the things in my mind, they first and foremost must address the one thing that is competing for my sensory attention.

Interest as a Requirement for Focusing

Less predictable was the idea that interest not only allowed for focus, but was an actual requirement of it. This seemed like a "no brainer" at first —don't we all focus better when we are interested? With that belief in my head, I must admit, it wasn't until I heard the same thing ten times over that I began to suspect that there might be something different going on within interests and focus for those who were helping me with the study.

As a reasonably good student and scholar myself, I would say that I have had a much easier time focusing on something when I have found it interesting. But during one of my ASD expert professional interviews, as the participant was detailing the alignment between focus and interest, this possibility finally dawned on me: perhaps for those with ASD, they can't actually focus well at all on those things that are not within some narrow band of interest.

I posed this topic for discussion with several of the participants and one confirmed this by sending me a study that he had seen on the topic of focus and interest in autism. The specific "why" for focusing difference came later, because it really took me some time to deeply understand how, given all the energy that is required to compensate for multiple cognitive differences, people with autism find it incredibly exhausting to focus on areas that are undeveloped. The primary statements that I felt most closely aligned with this particular *aha* moment follow.

I can concentrate for long periods of time while researching a topic which I find very interesting, and I feel intelligent in the areas of general knowledge that I am interested in.

I've always considered myself an "information junkie," having an insatiable desire to learn about things which really interest me.

Others seem to be able to focus to some degree even if it does not particularly interest them. I can't. I need the energy that comes from being "in the zone"—doing something that I enjoy and find interesting to be able to compensate and focus at all.

Using a gas tank analogy, I might only have one gallon a day for things that don't interest me, but it seems that I have a full tank for things that do interest me.

Focus, Interest, and Perseveration

Still trying to stick to my training, I next created an attention category, but as that theme emerged, the data suggested that autism was not specifically associated with attentional difficulties. Rather, focus, interests, and perseverations drove attention.

Within this topic, the central idea emerged that focus is certainly much less taxing when interest-based. I reiterate the following points to help the reader understand how I determined that focus also relates to sensory processing, memory, and ultimately, cognitive performance.

I've always felt anxious about learning things for which I have little interest. I often just can't do it at all unless I can find something in it that interests me. If I am not in some way intellectually engaged, then I just shut down and it is like my thinking for that topic stops.

Most of the people with autism I know who have been able to incorporate their interests into a successful career were very fortunate. My interests were never in line with what someone who was hiring actually wanted, so I have been forced to take a number of part-time, menial jobs to support myself. When working menial jobs that don't interest me, I fatigue quickly. I just don't have enough energy to keep doing something that isn't interesting to me.

I find that I need to keep things very simple to avoid the need to multi-task. I am very good at breaking things down, but find it difficult to make my choices and focus on one thing that doesn't much interest me. It reminds me a lot of a big equation in algebra, how it breaks down. I have a lot of boundaries in place so I can keep focus in the one place I need it most, and to do this, I go for the simple and the thing that interests me if I can.

Apparently, we can have autism and other learning disabilities also. I believe that I struggle with something a bit like attention deficit disorder, although I don't think that I experience it in exactly the same way as others who are not also autistic. I don't seem to have any problems with being impulsive, or even paying attention, and I can focus for hours on some small aspect of a thing that interests me. I struggle to pay attention to certain things, especially when I don't find them interesting. My organizational skills are also pretty darn abysmal.

Memory

When I conducted the literature review for my doctoral research, I reviewed hundreds of studies. The finding that stood out across all the research on cognitive difference in autism was consensus that those with autism often had "prodigious memory." Although I had never learned about this specifically in my clinical training, I thought back on the kids I had known through the years. While not very many of them tested well on the working memory indexes of the IQ tests, I had heard over and over that memory was a strength by those who knew them well. In fact, memory for specific detail stood out as one of the most common statements that I had heard from parents of children with autism across my twenty-five-year career. In many cases, strength in remembering was reported with shock as parents relayed how remarkable their child's memory skills for certain things really was. I then thought back to clinical reports from all the savant studies, and in spite of the other savant skills being studied, every one of the savant reports had also referred to "prodigy" within memory.

Even for one of the "lowest-functioning" nonverbal clients in my own practice, I recall the special education teacher telling me that "there is something really unusual about his memory, because he can look at a completed puzzle, turn it upside down (so the picture part was on the floor), then take all the pieces apart and put them back together with no trial and error, by simply having remembered the position of the pieces." This young man could apparently reassemble the pieces "almost as fast as he had taken them apart." This memory skill held true even when staff members took the pieces apart and mixed them up by placing them into the box. This young man had apparently memorized the spatial position of every puzzle piece in the box for approximately five different 250-piece puzzles in his classroom. Yet as a ninth grade student, he couldn't speak, he couldn't feed himself using utensils, and he couldn't dress himself or use the toilet independently.

This skill appears related in some way to visual-spatial memory. But I have also known those with prodigious number memory: one child I worked with had memorized the number sequence in pi for 1,000 digits, and others could remember and re-read books or even encyclopedias as if they were holding the book in their hands.

Some of the initial statements about memory and its ties to the other categories seem best summarized in the statements that follow.

Memory. Ah, I remember it well. I have always had a very good memory for what might be called "extraneous" facts surrounding a particular circumstance, so if I see an actor in a show and I can't immediately remember where I saw them before, I will be able to remember that they were wearing a green sweater previously or had blond hair. Not a lot of help at first in working out where I have seen them before, but every little bit eventually helps.

I have noticed that my memory does compensate for deficits in other areas. For example, as I stated, I have a problem with fluency. It is really a hindrance to my ability to express myself. However, my good memory helps me to retain a large amount of information and a good vocabulary with which I can compensate.

I have always been interested, obsessed even, with and can easily remember facts and the provenance of facts (where they came from). I think these help me relate to the world.

I have an exceptional memory for specifics, sort of within this narrow window; but within my "window of memory," I can recall every detail to the degree that I can often re-experience the memory and sometimes even pick up on details that I missed when I was actually there. On the other hand, I don't remember the general aspects across all "windows," as I think others seem to do.

For me, all my memories are quite specific and relate to the particular, versus this broader set of "fuzzy abstracts."

I am able to successfully compartmentalize my memories in ways that I don't think others are able to do. Because I do this, I sometimes feel as if I only exist in the here and now, that my memory for the past might not actually exist, although in my thinking mind, I can rationally remember that it must.

While we all seem to have very sophisticated sense-based and/or visual-based memory systems, we don't all seem to have the ability to easily remember language. I am likely to remember everything about a particular situation except for what was said.

Specific in Detail Yet Narrow in Focus

As I reviewed these statements, I was able to confirm that every one of the individuals in the study identified certain aspects of memory as a cognitive strength. Several articulated that their long-term memory and not their short-term memory was advanced. This was combined for me with another story I heard told by an autism expert. This individual stated that when she remembered a church steeple, she remembered each one she had ever seen, in very specific detail, across all the individual church steeples she had ever seen in her entire life. As I thought about that, even though I have seen countless church steeples, I have in my mind, even now, a vague image off in the distance of one single church steeple set against a cloudless blue sky. That is my only complete visual memory for the topic "church steeple." This forced me to ask the question, "Why do those with ASD seem to have countless, independent, and fully developed memories for a multitude of different church steeples, when I only have one?"

From there, I was able to piece together sentences and phrases on this topic to suggest that perhaps in ASD, a different memory system than my own (and for most NT people I know) might be in effect. According to what I was hearing, the ASD memory system is highly intensified, very narrow in topic, extremely detailed and complete, and not generalizable. What I mean by this last part is that because things are remembered with such rich and specific detail for those with autism, they are not generalized to other memories like them; people with autism remember the specific differences, not the things that are the same.

Statements in the section that follow also include personal theories about how memory is reinforced by sensory information and by interests for those with ASD. The concluding statements in this section seem to also explain how senses, relationships, and interests strengthen an already sophisticated, long-term memory system.

I get that I am a sponge. I have really, really good memory. Especially when I was a kid, I had a memory that just wouldn't quit. I seemingly remembered absolutely everything.

I have an especially strong long-term memory, although my short-term memory isn't as good. At this point in my life, my long-term memory is much better than my short-term memory, but I think my memory is quite exceptional.

Short-term memory is more difficult for us. It seems to me that memory and sensory processing are tied together because the stronger a sensation, is the more memorable it becomes. The way I can see memories, feel them, even sometimes smell and taste them allows me to immerse myself in them, relive them, and remember them forever.

I pretty much remember anything that I find interesting. People like me remember certain kinds of verbal facts, but we also seem to access and remember sensory data more easily. Ask me if I remembered to lock my door, and I'll think back to when I left my room and play back the sensory log. Do I recall the feeling of my hand reaching into my bag, pulling out the key, and turning it in the lock?

Language memory is very useful for interacting with others, but entirely unnecessary for most tasks. People who think like me seem to remember a more complete sensory experience, which we find more useful.

When I was eleven years old, my mother and I went to Switzerland to visit friends of the family. While there, we traveled by train down to Italy to visit my cousin who was living there at the time. At the end of the visit he took us to the station in Milan, but somehow, we got on the wrong train. Instead of heading straight toward the Alps as we should have, we were going back to Switzerland—we were traveling parallel. I tried pointing this out to my mother, but she wasn't about to take advice from me. Eventually, she figured out we were going in the wrong direction and we got off the train in a town called Chives. I remember it was cold and rainy and, for some reason, I never forgot the name of that town. I also remember everything about it just like it was yesterday. We were there only briefly waiting for a train back to Milan, I wasn't keeping a diary, and I don't think I made any conscious effort to commit it to memory; but there it is, and the fact that I can remember something like that with that much detail totally astounds people. If I could draw, I could literally draw a picture of that town with every single detail as it was on that day.

If we compare memory in autism to serial versus parallel bus ports on a computer, I find it explains memory in the following way: a deliberate listener/observer watching for a specific "car" will cease watching once they have seen the car they are looking for. On a single lane road, that will be a single car (referring to a serial port and the way he sees NTs processing); all subsequent cars will be disregarded. But on an eight-lane road (referring to a parallel bus port, the previous discussion of sensory processing difference, and an eight-lane highway system of sensory processing difference for those with ASD), the sought-after car can be a member of a group of cars. In my case, and for those like me, the car I am looking for and the other cars in the same group will all end up in short-term memory and fade quickly. But if at a later time (while watching for the same car), any of the other cars re-appear in the group with the car I am looking for, their memory will be reinforced (as being connected to the first car). If there is no repeat of cars, their occurrence will fade as well, but the connections between repeating cars will be reinforced and remembered for a very long time.

Apart from originally sought information, the information that "sticks" for me would be that which is novel, interesting, odd, or disturbing.

As I read through the transcript of comments on memory, I discovered that what these individuals were describing as a very sophisticated and complete memory system for the specific was also riddled with holes for the general. In this next section, I highlight how thinking, remembering specifics, and even remembering something from an altered point of view is possibly the result of a very specific and detailed system of remembering that does not generalize across multiple concepts or ideas.

This is a general issue for us; we are often not able to remember something at the same time as we are thinking about it. Even though I have an excellent memory, I find that my memory has very some unusual holes.

I have an exceptional memory, but it has these gaping pieces missing in in it. When I remember my childhood experiences, I often remember them from a very specific vantage point and sometimes that memory is very different than the memory of someone else who was there with me. I might have focused on the pattern of the carpet and remembered it with exquisite detail, while my mom and dad focused on the therapist who was talking to our family about my behavior at school.

I often remember a very narrow point of view, even though I remember it in complete detail. Sometimes my sole memory for a situation is not at all relevant for others or even in line with what they remembered. In many instances my memories for a situation, even though they are incredibly detailed, are not very useful.

I remember the things that were important to me, although this often causes me to miss the memories that were important to others.

As I tried to piece together all the aspects of memory, I began to wonder if there were differences between verbal and visual memories. In other words, did those with verbal learning styles have good verbal memory, while those with visual learning styles struggled with verbal memory? Even less clear to me was how verbal versus visual memory works for those who have a very visual-spatial (able to easily see three-dimensional objects in their mind's eye) learning style.

So, I scanned my data for the topic of learning style and memory and found that memory wasn't the same for everyone with autism, as I had first suspected. But I did see a reoccurring theme: strong sensory-based memory was to be linked to nearly perfect memory (albeit narrowly focused and sometimes not focused on the things others are attending to). Visual memory also appears strong for everyone in the study, but the ability to remember sounds or words was not consistent. Below are some of the statements about difference in memory that came out of my research.

People who think like me seem to remember a more complete sensory experience easily. I think we also have strong visual memory in certain ways, but we don't all have the same ability to remember verbal information.

I'm actually terrible at trivia, but my visual memory is better than my verbal memory by quite a bit.

My memory is very visual; I remember things better if I see them, rather than if I only hear them. I have a surprisingly hard time remembering what I hear, especially in the short-term. I just remember things better if I see them.

I often think in three-dimensional images, except if I am remembering what I read in a book or on a piece of paper, then I see the page. I can easily read a page from a book in my mind as if I am reading the actual page (this from an individual who didn't read at all until he was almost eleven).

Many years ago, when I was living in Hawaii, I was playing a Trivial Pursuit-type game with friends called "Trivia-Aloha." The question was, "What is the state bird of Hawaii?" My mind went to the "H" volume of the set of *World Book Encyclopedia* that we had as kids. In my mind, I flipped the pages to "Hawaii." I searched the top of one page, where they showed the state tree, state flower, and found the state bird. I saw the page in my memory, then I answered the question.

In addition to strong sensory-based memory, I also have good spatial memory. I once knew that a certain cabinet-level official in one country where I served was out of favor, because he did not stand where he normally did at an official meeting. I literally have a photographic visual memory.

I can see things in pictures so well that I can see Shakespeare in front of me now and I can actually read the words on the page as if I were holding the book.

I have an almost photographic memory for maps and can navigate anywhere having seen a map of the terrain of a particular area. I can just spatially orient myself to the terrain and follow the map.

Oddly enough, I sometimes don't think my visual memory is that great, or perhaps it is too great, because I miss details which are right in front of my nose because they are slightly different from what I was expecting within my memory. I have seen children make the same sort of mistakes, but never other adults.

I don't think I have a very good visual memory at all for short-term things. But visual details, things that interest me visually, I can remember these things forever. Sounds and words are also written in stone in my memory.

My strong memory for sound is useful for pop music trivia but not much else. I can easily see musical scores in my head, though, so I guess that is a kind of visual memory.

If it is possible to have a near photographic memory for sounds, that would be it. When replaying a song in my head, I often come across an aspect of it that I was not consciously aware of when I actually listened to it, like a drum beat or horn flare. At first I thought my mind must have added the sound, but when I returned to the original recording and listened again, sure enough, there it was.

CHAPTER SEVEN

Compartmentalization of Memory and Object Permanence

In trying to understand memory, I accidentally stumbled on another topic that truly surprised me. With the help of a volunteer from Australia, I began to understand that in autism, because the memory system is so specific, sensory-rich, and yet compartmentalized and grounded in the singular (versus the general), that memories of an entire life or person can become lost. More than one of the participants described an experience similar to the discussion below about the "lost wife." As I considered various aspects of this topic, I realized how remarkably confusing it could potentially be for young children with autism who have forgotten some important aspect of home, family, school, or friendships.

I think because I have such strong memory, I can compartmentalize my memories very easily. I think I sort of pack up some areas of memory, then I lose them.

Lost memories cause me to struggle with what I believe most would call "object permanence." I think our problems with object permanence were especially relevant for some of us when we were young.

Sometimes when I travel and I have been away for a few weeks, I can't quite remember what my wife's face looks like. Because of that, I have a hard time remembering for certain whether she is real or not. I have found that it helps to see a picture of her face to make her feel real to me and to help bring me back to my memories of home.

When I am away from home for some time, I can't always really remember if I have another life. I am just in the life I am in. But when I get home, then that set of memories opens up, and I can't easily remember the broader aspects of my trip; although I can usually remember, in great detail, some of the specific details.

Although deeply tied to the previous idea, as I thought about compartmentalization and narrow bands of memory for those with autism, I felt that the next statements added an additional dimension. While my mind has the statements that follow linked in some way, I'm not sure I can even now articulate these relationships fully. I'm also quite certain that because my own memories are not compartmentalized, I don't really have a sense of the altered passage of time that those with ASD explained. I simply don't have these experiences. But this topic did help me figure out how memories might be reinforced and stored for at least some people on the spectrum.

I believe that our deficits in short-term memory lead us to an inability to process certain types of data in real time, unspoken social cues as an example. The outworking of this would be a seeking of predictability so that you are relying on long-term memory to interpret the world, rather than relying on sense memory/short-term memory for your speed of processing.

When I was a kid, I could stare at something for hours and not know it had been hours. I do have a strong association with other times in memory; I can remember them like they just happened.

If I hear a song, I might have a very strong, full-body sensation about the store I went to in 1979 where I first heard that song, and that brings me back to that time and place such that I can re-live that experience completely, sometimes to the point of losing track of what I am doing in the here and now.

When I am reading a story, the time around me almost feels like it stops. It's like I have to stop and intentionally pull myself back into the real world and reorient; even when I stop reading, I might not still be clear which world I am in.

My memory for certain things is so rich and vivid that when I recall a memory, it is almost like jumping from place to place, or time to time. I can actually be at the place I am remembering, with all of my sensory experiences of that place intact.

Most people don't get that memory for us is not just an emotional attachment to a particular time, it's actually physical, a full sensorial experience. It can be really enjoyable or exciting, but it has its downsides. I seem to be pretty well rooted in my reality now, but I didn't always have a good sense of passage of time when I was younger, and I sometimes lost track of where I was or what was actually real.

I am sometimes made aware of how time escapes me. I once played guitar at a pizzeria and I was running a video for promotional purposes. When I watched back through the video, I realized that I had no idea that this person had said goodnight three times before I even answered. I just lost that time within everything that was going on around me. I think it just takes such a high level of concentration for me to do certain things that time and memory kind of pass without my awareness.

Real or Created in Memory?

When bringing all the thoughts together within this section, I was reminded of a client who had created a very real imaginary friend in her late teens. Her memory descriptors for this "person" were so vivid that, at first, I believed she was suffering from a thought disorder. But as I got to know her more, she was entirely grounded in the present and never believed her imaginary friend to be real, even though she had created such a vivid experience that she remembered her as if she were real. Her memory for this relationship was so vivid in her imagination that she was able to create complete sensory experiences with this "friend," and these were so rich in their detail that my client even felt grief when she finally decided to let her imagery friend leave.

Patterns and Visual Details

With what I felt amounted to really significant cognitive difference in both memory and focus, I was curious to understand how these played out within the deeper levels of abstract reasoning and thought for the volunteers in my study. So, as I dug deeper, I began to specifically explore deep patterns of cognitive difference within various aspects of visual information processing. As I did this, a clear trend seemed to emerge for strength in seeing and recognizing visual patterns. This was especially apparent when I contrasted this strength against what I had previously discovered about learning styles. For a time, I anticipated that I might even be able to categorize these strengths within either visual or verbal style differences, but what I learned surprised me. Even when I accounted for extreme differences in both sensory processing and learning style, I still found a common thread within every participant in the study: an uncanny ability to see or sense patterns and rhythms. Other cognitive strengths also appeared as universals, and these included the ability to "see" the problem, attention to visual detail, and deep sensory or visual thinking (even in those who were "verbal facts people"). Here's what the volunteers had to say about their cognitive strengths in visual pattern recognition and the ability to attend to visual details.

Based on what I have talked about with other people on the spectrum, we are incredibly skilled in specific things, but we also have extremely specific deficiencies. I think neurotypicals have access to the bank of knowledge that is used by those of us who are on the spectrum. But I think something happened to us that caused a fracturing and gave us this unique ability to do different stuff, sometimes at the expense of other things.

I have a good ability to analyze disparate information and come to a conclusion that is correct. I guess you could say I am gifted in my nonverbal capacity. My ability to see things that other people can't is quite unusual. I see super specific details.

My autism increases my ability to acquire information and it increases my ability to take disparate pieces and create an abstract form that other people can't conceive or visualize. I am especially strong at problem solving and visual pattern recognition.

Visual patterns are definitely a strength area for me. I also have above average attention to visual detail. Seeing patterns, linear thinking, spotting ambiguity, these are my strengths.

For a job, I was once given a programming task to process some files. The input files were for some kind of genomic sequencing project. I don't know who or what generated them, but I was able to look at what appeared to be random symbols and see a pattern, and that pattern showed me what my program should do.

My friend is a theorist in high energy particle physics, and I remember when he would come back from Harvard and we would have these conversations; he would say, "I know you are just an artist, but I have better conversations with you than I do with the physicists, because they often can't see these things." I can easily see time and space, light, frequencies, and wave particles so physics makes perfect sense, because I can visualize it. It's what I naturally see.

Freeze-Frame Recall

While all the volunteers described strengths in their pattern recognition and discrimination for visual detail, as I explored visual information processing further, I found another trend that wasn't shared by all. I learned that for some of those who had identified themselves with the "visual or sensorial" learning style, they could also glance at something out of the corner of the eye, then see it in "freeze-frame" (as if a single event had been photographed using a rapid lens, but within a series of independent, still images). For two of the members in this group, the "freezing" of a visual image sequence came with the ability to stop, slow down, or even speed up the images of an event, then replay them later, frame-by-frame. One person used this to explain why watching a movie was somewhat difficult for him. Based on the data from this group, "verbal facts people" are less likely to do this. Here's how this visual difference was explained.

Another wrinkle in figuring us out is one that happened not too long ago. I had a glass of water on the counter and I accidentally knocked the glass off with my arm. Here is what I experienced. I knew I felt my arm on the glass, I knew the glass was gone. The next thing I knew, I had a photographic, freeze-frame set of pictures of the glass falling. It was like still photography. It wasn't like a video. I could see the glass midair with water coming out sideways, at all these different stages and angles until it hit the floor.

One of my skills is that I can look at a glance, retain what I see, and then freeze everything in still images and replay it all later in a set of fixed images in front of me. I can then replay these strings of still images at any speed I want to.

I have had moments where I have seen a person enter the room and, while they are in motion, I can go through a series of actions in my mind from the past. Like taking a group of pictures, I can see their movements, frame by frame, before these actually happen.

Even though I am very visual, I sometimes need to watch a movie several times to figure out the plot. I think I just see so much more than what the producer of the film intends for me to see. It's why I don't see movies in the theater. I need to see every frame, frame by frame. I can do this in my day-to-day, but movies go too fast.

Spatial and Perceptual Differences

While there was a clear pattern of strength for certain aspects of visual information processing in all the study's volunteers, another big difference in the group showed up in the area of visual-spatial reasoning. Specifically, while members of this group could easily attend to visual details and see patterns within visual information sequences, they were seemingly polar opposites within their visual-spatial abilities. The "strong verbal facts people" reported significant challenges with visual-spatial problem solving, while those who were both visual and sensorial in their learning style reported nearly perfect three-dimensional, spatial problem-solving abilities. The sentences and phrases that I believe most strongly support these conclusions are listed in the following narrative and include several interesting statements about how individuals in the study viewed these unique differences.

Well, I could give you an example of visual thinking correctly applied in cognition. When I was in the army, they would run a betting pool to see how fast I could get from one particular point to another point. They would show me a topographical map, then blindfold me and take me out—it could be any distance—and drop me off. With no map and no compass, I could take that landscape in front of me and lift it up and turn it, then take the map I had seen and articulate its height and spin it in all the directions. From just that, I could figure out exactly where my orientation in space was and, without missing a step, I could find my way back to the base.

In many cases I often don't need a compass, because I can just figure out the direction I need to go.

Women on the spectrum that I know seem to have a high prevalence of problems navigating in cars or getting to locations. I have wondered if there is some chromosomal function to the particular visual-spatial tasks of navigation.

I hear of some ASD people reporting that they need to plan out trips well in advance and rehearse their travel. Many of us don't like GPS because it is so confusing and stressful. I have always been told that I am a very good abstract problem solver. This feels accurate.

Part-to-Whole Processing

With clear differences between people in their deeply abstract spatial reasoning, I suspected another area of difference in the ways in which these individuals ordered and built meaning for new information. While I knew they were all primarily visual in their sequencing (the way they glued their thoughts together), I didn't suspect that they also would be part-to-whole in their logic. In this area, I found an additional trend for similarity; at least for those in this group, every one of them needed to assemble enough parts of a particular concept to create a meaningful whole. Once they did that, they could then deeply understand it. But, unlike most neurotypical people, the parts and pieces they needed to create the whole were incredibly specific and detailed.

One individual described his fascination with fans as a child, and in this discussion, he talked about how he needed to know every brand, every motor style, every wood or plastic type possible for the blades, every finish for the metal, and fully understand the way that the blade tilt adjustments affected air movement. Until he had all of this information assembled, he could not fully comprehend what a fan actually was.

I believe now that what this individual was trying to explain is that in autism, until enough parts are present to construct a comprehensive whole, understanding is lost. This is better explained in the following statements.

I have to piece together a full set of what might seem to others as seemingly unrelated details, but once I do that, I can easily see the big picture.

If I have to learn a new programming language, I do this by reading lots and lots of specific examples of how the language is used; eventually I can construct something original, a big picture, out of the parts I've learned, then I have learned the language.

I learn by going from the specific to the general. This is sometimes a weakness. When I was little, I remember asking my father how to tell if an animal was a dog. Dogs come in all different sizes and shapes, they can have very different fur from one another, and they smell different. His answer was they just have this "doggy look." I finally constructed the general concept of "doggy look" over years and years of specific encounters with different kinds of dogs. Until I did this I really could not grasp "doggy."

Because I am wired to hyper-focus on the specific, and this allows me to form a more complete big picture, I can't move forward until my picture is complete. I have a hard time seeing the parts or steps, and I get overwhelmed when I try to think about them all together. Once I have assembled a "whole," I no longer feel confused.

When staring something new, I learn best when I work from a series of small, specific examples. Once I have accumulated enough of these to form the big picture, then I can envision the outcome or result.

I am great at big-picture stuff once I fully understand a thing, but I need my staff to write memos for me for all the little day-to-day things, and I need the big picture assembled before I can function. Once the details are all spelled out for me, I can relax. Otherwise, I feel kind of lost.

I think most people can see the little steps needed to complete a task, but have a harder time forming the big picture. I can form the big picture easily once I understand everything about it, but I can't easily form the steps myself to get there.

Being able to see the big picture with this much detail is hard in a way, though, because I get overwhelmed by the details and steps that I will need to follow to get me there.

My ability to hyper-focus on the specific, recall details, recognize patterns and rhythms, and envision the big picture are pronounced attributes that should be useful (assuming the sensory environment isn't too over-stimulating) in many areas of science and technology.

Although not all those on the spectrum are like me, in addition to my visual skills of pattern recognition, I am able to quickly pick up on new languages—including regional dialects. These have given me a significant edge in my field. Once you understand the big picture about how all languages are created, learning a new one is easy.

The Effects of Sensory-Cognitive Difference on Social Interaction

This final aspect of autism had an immediate and obvious place in the narrative from the outset, and in fact, it is what most people think about first when they think about autism. Then again, isn't that just a part of our developmentally normal paradigm? Given clear indicators for social difference in the literature, I didn't want to miss these for this group, but I also didn't want them to take center stage. While thousands of studies have attempted to explain social skill deficits for those with ASD, what seemed to be missing in the literature to me was awareness about neurotypical bias and false perceptions about what is or is not normal within the social arena.

As I reviewed the thoughts and insights from my volunteers on the topic of social difference, what emerged was the idea that social interaction in autism is both a primary difference and a secondary result that has evolved out of the culmination of differences already discussed. For this reason, I chose to open my discussion on the topic of social difference with these statements.

I can only offer insight into my experience. It seems that the only data that might completely elude me is the social stuff of group dynamics. Sometimes that data just doesn't make sense TO ME, and other times I am convinced that it just doesn't make sense PERIOD!

I always tend to be in the minority. I'm either the only one who doesn't know what's going on or I'm the only one who does. Either way, it's problematic for me and viscerally frustrating for others.

I believe that we socially understand too much but recognize that most people are just not very authentic. This results in us placing less value on social things.

I find it useful to distinguish between physical reality and social reality when approaching a new situation. If it is purely physical reality, then

I would have no problem dealing with the slower-moving and repetition-tolerant issues which are likely to arise. However, social situations are fast-moving and not repetition-tolerant.

As I have learned more about brain functionality, I have learned that specific "modules" exist for processing different aspects of visual information and others for other sensory input. So, it occurred to me that given how important social groups are for our success as a species, a social processing module may well have evolved—like a math co-processing chip on a CPU. If this module did not function correctly, then it could explain why social functioning is so badly affected, while other apparently related functions, such as general IQ or visual information processing, might not be.

Our social problem lies in a specific part of the general processing engine rather than in a general aspect of it. In the past, I have tried to explain my social deficits within the context of the brain as a general information processing engine. My explanation sort of makes sense if you assume that there is something about social signal processing which is particularly labor intensive.

I used to believe that our social difficulties arose out of the sheer speed at which social signals appear and disappear. You barely have time to notice that an eyebrow has been lifted or a tone of voice has changed before it has gone and been replaced with other signals. You certainly don't have time to ponder what the signal might mean. As I have gotten older, I realize it is even more complicated than I first thought, because so many different skills are required within the social dynamic.

My current view on social skills in autism is to compare autism to sickle cell anemia in evolutionary terms. A low level of it is protective, even beneficial, to the group as a whole. For example, everyone benefits when an autistic's "genius" discovers a new law of physics or invents something useful. However, too much and it becomes detrimental to both the individual and the society. However, the group is not badly affected by these individuals as they do not socialize much, and they tend not to breed. Tough for the individual, though!

Standing under bright fluorescent lights, smiling at people, and having to be social is not really my skill set, so I have had to work a series of low-paying jobs and have learned to live frugally. The things that I have had to do to survive seem socially odd to most people.

Bullying

Within the social domain, those in the study who talked about socialization expressed a variety of heart-breaking stories that certainly affected how they believed they had evolved socially. Most had been teased and bullied, many by the adults (even teachers) in their lives. This had resulted in them taking a position of self-preservation and self-protection. One of the participants shared how the ability to discern from good versus bad people had also developed. Segments from these stories follow.

I have always struggled with reading body language, although I didn't know I struggled with it when I was young.

As a kid, I knew that most people had a way of communicating that didn't rely on words and I knew I was not privy to that; I didn't know what it was, I had no idea. When I was young, I heard all these people talking about how I didn't read body language. I remember wondering what people meant by reading body language. I thought about it a lot, but I just couldn't figure it out.

Not picking up on social cues leads to isolation and vulnerability, which is picked up early on. If you then perform better academically than those who are more socially adept, it just makes matters worse.

Young kids with autism may not fully understand the downside or "underbelly" of group dynamics until it targets them. I learned quickly that I needed to avoid certain social situations for self-preservation. I was targeted since I started elementary school, so now I am very aware of potential issues and I understand the importance of protecting myself.

For me, everything really came crashing down in high school, where the unwritten social rules become so much more complex. In the late 70s, with undiagnosed Asperger's and a world that didn't have a clue about autism, it was all I could do to keep attending school—let alone concentrate enough to get decent grades. I did eventually manage to graduate, but it wasn't until five years later that I started college.

During the worst of my school years I developed an eating disorder, which began when I was about fourteen. It was a means of self-medicating back then, but it is still an issue to this day.

It's like I am a criminal investigator. I look at certain patterns of behavior, speech, and language, and I put all these pieces together to give me a framework of who an individual is. Now I can usually get a pretty good idea about a person and what benefit or harm they might have for me from about five minutes of watching them and talking to them. That wasn't true when I was younger.

Challenges with Social Communication

As a subtopic beneath the broader discussion about social differences, some of the same challenges with communication that were reported in the cognitive difference category rolled over into the social arena. However, and in addition, certain attributes of communication difficulty were specific and unique to the social arena. These specifics are highlighted within the following statements:

I think that my language processing speed is probably the biggest problem for me socially. Being able to ... it's just sort of this need to express myself all the time. I don't always know when to start or stop talking and I am quite unskilled at inserting myself into a conversation already in progress. The other issue is not knowing when it is my turn to talk in a group.

For me, it is the fluency. Often when I am trying to communicate with others, my brain has already marched on, so it takes a while for the words to catch up; but most people are not really that patient.

When I first started my professional career, I had a boss who said to me, "You only talk to people one-on-one. You don't ever talk to people in a group, so people don't see you as very social." Which I thought was very odd. I hadn't noticed that other people were any different than I was.

I don't often talk in groups, I talk to an individual, then another individual, then another individual. I don't really understand how people interact in a group.

I find that I need to ask a lot of questions to try to work out what is going on in a conversation and I can't do that in a group situation. I appreciate that other people find my questions irritating or even insulting, but the answers I get from others when I ask, even though they might seem trivial or obvious, are usually necessary for me to work out what is important (and therefore true) to the person with whom I am speaking.

I don't lie or improvise easily. I think neurotypical people often do that without thinking, so they can more easily move the conversation along or extract themselves from it when it no longer interests them.

Reading Body Language

Although not universal, most of the people with autism that I have known, both in and outside of my research, have also reported significant challenges with reading and interpreting non-verbal information. Those who did not feel this was an issue were remarkably on the opposite side of it and more than one of them described their abilities to read nonverbal cues and body language as nearly "empathic." Within this range, some responded to topics of nonverbal cues by discussing their choices to interact mostly with friends. Others emphasized that the value others put on social interaction might be overly high. In other words, as important as socialization might seem to the rest of us, social difference isn't necessarily that important or necessary to at least some people with autism. One of the participants re-tells a story where nonverbal communication was blamed for something else: the dishonesty of fellow employees. Last, participants reiterate that sometimes the cost of the energy required for social interactions simply outweighs the benefit. The range of difference I found on the topic of reading social cues and body language for those who volunteered for my research are represented in the statements that follow.

I think I understand sometimes if someone is very angry or really happy, but I don't always understand why. For example, someone might be angry with me, but I might not know the reason. Do some people know why people get mad at them?

I don't know social things innately. I have been married (now divorced) and I have kids, but to be honest I really don't know what to do now, at this time in my life, to initiate a relationship with someone. I can't flirt. I don't know if someone has ever flirted with me. I just don't know the rules. It's just foreign to me, completely foreign.

Certainly, across that whole area of human experience, I can't read it and I don't know enough to imitate social things successfully. I can't fake it. I think I also lack the ability to imitate social things successfully, even when I sort of intellectually understand what people might prefer I do in a certain situation.

My experience has been that there have been times where, if I had the ability to process nonverbal cues, it would have been beneficial to me. If you cannot work out the subtleties of someone's facial expression until hours after the conversation is over, then you can effectively be considered to not be reading their nonverbal cues.

I was in one job and periodically we receive an assessment by the leadership of the post. I remember my supervisor told me, "You are doing great and people like you, but you don't really walk around or talk to people. In a leadership position, walking around is kind of important." So, I decided I would try walking around and talking to the other employees. But then, for the next assessment, my supervisor said, "People really didn't like you walking around and talking to them. It made them feel very uncomfortable." I was obviously doing something wrong, but I had no idea what it was. I think when I try to act "normal" socially, it just comes off wrong.

Reading body language is sometimes ambiguous. It doesn't mean we can't do it, though. It's just that often we find people's body language to be inconsistent or even inaccurate. People try to convey that they are fine when they are not, for example.

My conflict resolution skills are something I am still learning about over these past several years. When I was younger, conflict made me feel very unsure of myself and socially very awkward. Now I am more sure of myself, but conflict is still so unpleasant to have to deal with that I deliberately try to avoid it at all costs. This isn't always a good thing.

I can't always see social problems coming. Sometimes I am just too distracted, or I am focused on other things. But if I have the energy and I can force myself to focus on the social, then I can almost always figure it out.

When we have the energy, we are fully capable of understanding and recognizing emotion in ourselves and others. We don't lack the skill, although sometimes we lack the desire.

I think figuring out social things is easier when you take the emotional out. It sounds kind of weird, but I am actually pretty good at reading people. I can observe and understand people's expressions and figure out what they might be feeling in most cases.

I've always been almost empathic, at times, in that I can figure out what people are feeling, even though I don't always pick up on the things you might call body language. I think I must use a different system to know how people feel, because I can't rely on what I see in facial expressions, but I still just know without really thinking about it too much how they are feeling.

I'm exceptionally good at reading emotions in animals. My pets don't try to cover up what they are feeling so I can read them easily. Once I learned to do that, I could apply the same strategy to most people, unless they were being deceptive.

I'm not sure if my ability to read people is a natural thing or something I have learned from social skills classes. But I am surprisingly pretty good at it if I want to be. Being able to observe and understand people's expressions and what they might be feeling is usually pretty clear to me.

In large, I would have to say that if I employ good strategies, my social skills really are not an issue, and that is why I say that my issue with nonverbal cues is *an* issue and not *the* issue. It isn't even close to being *the* issue. I think our challenges with social things are way overstated in terms of them being important.

I have found that if I only associate with high-quality people, then my issue with the nonverbal goes away. High-quality people are not looking for an excuse to throw a temper tantrum or be offended. High-quality people think before they emote, and all of my potential social problems go away when I am with them.

Being with friends is far and away the number one strategy that has always worked splendidly for me in dealing with the social. If I only hang out with people I know well, they know how to take me. If I do something odd, my friends don't automatically assume that I am trying to start a fight. They just know that I'm odd and that's okay with them.

Sometimes, things are blamed on my inability to read social cues when that has nothing to do with it. Let me tell you a story that I often tell when I talk to teachers about nonverbal cues. I had a job in the mid-90s where I was a service employee and I made a lot of tips—$6,000 in four months. It was a gravy train for me, and I was good at that job. When I was hired, my employer told me that I had to let the accountant know how many tips I got so they could withhold the taxes on my checks. I did that, but I did not see the problem coming; my co-workers were not pleased because they were not reporting nearly all of their tips. I thought you just had to do your job, follow the rules, and everything would be fine. Now I know better.

Most of the times that I have been rightly accused of having social skills problems were times when I was simply too cognitively spent to value the social over the other things in my life that were more important to me. Social interaction is particularly time-consuming and exhausting and I hate to say this, but I usually don't get that much out of it.

At this point in my journey, even though all my training had taught me to see social deficits as a core feature in autism, I came to understand that social difference in autism is simply just the culmination of all differences present in ASD. With this, I found it more important than ever to understand the recursive and interactive nature of the social dynamic for its relationship to all the other aspects of cognitive and sensory difference. The few remaining statements seemed to point to the interrelatedness of all things "autism" for their contribution to social difference. These statements follow.

There are certain types that I can't get along with. They are antagonistic and nasty and inauthentic and even though I try I just can't get along with them, so I have learned to protect myself from them. I recognize that there are people out there who can't tolerate me, who I am, or my quirkiness. They are not forgiving at all. But once I have recognized that in a person, I know to steer clear of them.

I see social interaction as a particularly labor-intensive activity in and of itself. But place me in a complex sensory environment, such as a cocktail party or a busy work setting, and force me to make small talk, and I just won't have enough energy to do it.

Even though I am quite verbal and I have a large vocabulary, my communication timing seems to set me apart socially. I have a few close friends and quite honestly that is enough for me. When I am with my friends, I communicate more easily, my sensory needs are respected, and I am in my tribe.

Remarkably, this point closed the circle and brought me back to my beginning. As I tried to consider my own thinking about autism through a new and different lens, one that gave possibility to the fact that there might be many ways to function differently and still be "normal," I was forced to come down off my high horse and ask the question, "I wonder what they (people with autism) think of those who don't have autism?" The answer to my question was right in front of me.

Most neurotypical people strike me as having big areas of cognitive disconnect. There are adjectives that are often hurled in my direction that are actually more descriptive of the accuser, but they don't seem to realize it. For example, one that I get a lot is that I am arrogant. I'll put this as simply as I know how, I do not insist that everyone needs to be exactly like me, but other people, especially people in groups, do insist that I have to be exactly like them. Which one of these is arrogant? To me, the level of arrogance in most people is astonishing. They don't view themselves as arrogant, they view me as charity.

The attempts of others to force me to be like them are viewed by them as the equivalent of raising me up. From my perspective, I don't want to be dragged down to their level. The gossip, the dishonesty, the temper tantrums, the back-stabbing, I don't want to be around that stuff and I don't want to be victimized by it. But it's even more profound than that it is not just their behaviors that are problematic, I find most people to be intellectually offensive.

The actions of others who are supposed to be intelligent just seem to be beneath any level of human intelligence that I can imagine. I would not want to live if I had to live like that. Many neurotypical people seem to behave in ways that, to me, seem beneath any level of human intelligence, with their bullying, gossiping, and dishonesty. There is a lot of darkness that goes along with social integration and being "normal."

People may call me robotic, but their behavior is strikingly robotic to me. No matter how bad people feel or how rotten their day is, they say, "I'm fine, how are you?" That does not even feel human to me.

People say I am like a robot or that I'm not that smart because my emotions are informed by my thinking, because I don't know how to emote. For most people, it seems they emote first then think better of it later. I don't like the idea of replacing thinking with emotions. To me, thinking should inform emotions. Isn't thinking more intelligent than responding emotionally?

NTs often remind me of the Borg Collective on *Star Trek*. I don't want to be a "sheeple."

Others can do all this stuff, but they don't seem to be able to think for themselves. A couple of weeks ago, the special education teacher I was presenting with was explaining why it was hard to get kids with autism to stand in line, saying it was their sensory issues. Then she turned to me and I said, "The reason I don't like to stand in line is because I am not a cow. I don't want to be herded."

"Intelligent" is also sometimes used to mean other things, such as "socially compliant," which I am not. I think, for us, cognition and intelligence are independent of each other.

Sometimes people tagged me as not very intelligent because my life isn't characterized by many of the things that others are characterized by. But all of the classmates I grew up with have a pretty healthy amount of some (if not all) of the following: divorce lawyers, spousal maintenance, credit card debt, drug habits, convictions, etc.; I have zero of these. For me, it is just having the intelligence and wisdom to know from a young age that I just wouldn't be able to juggle it all.

We don't simply comply, even though we usually follow necessary rules. That might make us appear less intelligent. If everyone had autism, that could be a real problem for governments and social order.

Wisdom and Discernment

This opened the door to a final topic, which I found so remarkable that I will simply let those in the study explain it for themselves.

I think differently, I have a different experience of the world, and I am often not interested in the same things as other people. Is it any wonder, then, that my interactions and performance look different to those outside of my inner circle of comfort?

While I can try to explain my thinking to you, it really is so different from yours that you probably still won't be able to understand it. We simply don't define intelligence the same way at all, because my definition is heavily weighted in wisdom and common sense and has very little to do with your standard definitions about being smart.

My current view on autism is to compare it to sickle cell anemia in evolutionary terms. A low level of it is protective, even beneficial to the group as a whole. Everyone benefits when an autistic's "genius" discovers a new law of physics or invents something useful. Our excellent moral compasses would certainly be better for society. However, too much autism and it becomes detrimental to both the individual and the society.

Unlike most NT people, I don't mind if we don't agree; I find that disagreement can be kind of helpful. Sometimes different perspectives can have validity and present a clearer picture.

Our excellent moral compasses would certainly be better for society. I think that there needs to be a distinction between intelligence and wisdom or discernment. Discernment is often the byproduct of applied intelligence to the task of independent thinking. I think we Aspies often have very sophisticated levels of discernment.

To concludes the topic of cognitive difference, I created another SmartArt chart.

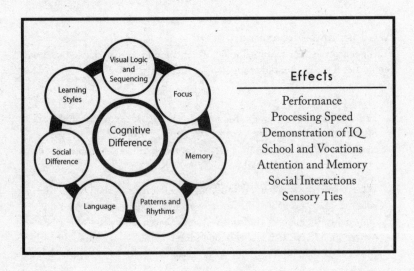

CHAPTER EIGHT

Cognition Reimagined: The Theory of Sensory Cognitive Difference

T he primary supporters of the neurodiversity movement have told us this: just as each and every plant and animal species on earth is necessary and essential to the complex biodiversity of our planet, the normal and natural cognitive differences that occur in humans are equally essential to the survival of the human race. I remember when I first read these words, I had just proposed my research topic to my doctoral committee and had been given the go-ahead to start my study. As I thought about this statement, my mind raced back through years of coursework and mountains of textbooks across my many years of education and I realized, perhaps for the first time, that since we humans first began classifying our world, we have worked very hard to order everything around us based on what we see and perceive as normal.

But what if, just as Galileo argued the Earth was not at the center of the universe, all our human thought—our classification systems, our developmental milestones, and our very definition about what is normal and what is not—somehow got it wrong? What if "normal, intelligent" humans are not actually at the center of the universe? Wouldn't it then be possible that those with ASD are not actually abnormal, broken, or intellectually lower functioning, but instead, because there is such a gap between their strengths and their deficits, they have just simply been misplaced in the realm of our human thought and acceptance for what intelligence actually is?

We know that success is defined by the culture and time in which one lives. So, isn't it possible that evolved intelligence accounts for at least some of what we see in those with autism? More specifically, is it possible that some aspect of autism will be needed for the future of our human race?

With these thoughts weighing heavily on in my mind, I began to wonder if there wasn't something particularly intelligent and wise about being on the autism spectrum—perhaps the world would be a better place if everyone had a touch of autism?

With what started out as a doctoral dissertation (rewritten for this book), I made the decision to study the topics of intelligence, cognition, and sensory processing with the help of seventeen diagnosed adults. You will recall that the original study behind this book was conducted with the intent of arriving at a more comprehensive theory within the cognitive-behavioral tradition to explain and more fully understand the core aspects of autism. Drawn from the insights and impressions of diagnosed individuals and joined with my own experiences—my work as a school psychologist and my experiences with a traumatic brain injury—I have now spent well over a thousand hours going through these topics and the statements I believe support them. Having now gone through everything twice (once for the dissertation and a second time for the book), I can honestly say that I believe to my core that the following statement, left as closely as possible in original words, most closely brings together the synthesis of my work. In the combined words of those diagnosed, the theory of sensory-cognitive difference is drawn from this statement.

Understand that, because of my significant sensory differences, I am on a different path. Because I am on a different path, I have different interests, make different observations, see different connections, and these differences dictate my focus. Because I focus on different things and I observe relationships between things differently, I remember different things and I remember them in a different way, which is often very specific but not usually very general. Because what I observe and remember about the world around me is different, I get to different places in my thinking and different things have value to me. I see patterns, oddities, and anomalies; I hear and sense rhythms; and within these I am sometimes even able to sense the metaphysical in ways that I think are unique to me and those like me. These cognitive differences are recursively tied to my sensory differences and often give way to how I think, feel, and sense. Combined, these give me a very different big picture about the world. As a result, I am cognitively evolved to be socially different, so that even though I may struggle to communicate my thoughts, I am very aware of the social and I would often rather observe than participate. I find social and cognitive value within those who accept me and fully appreciate me for all my differences. The person I am socially, how and what I think and value, what and how I remember, and what holds my interest and focus all influences how I perceive the world and process new sensory information, and over time, these differences have made me who I am: a very different yet completely whole individual.

The figure below depicts the culmination of the results of my research and gives a visual image to accompany what I would like to introduce as the theory of sensory-cognitive difference.

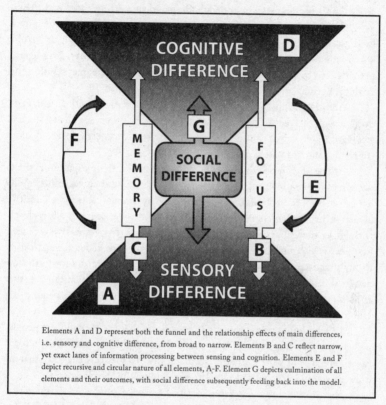

Elements A and D represent both the funnel and the relationship effects of main differences, i.e. sensory and cognitive difference, from broad to narrow. Elements B and C reflect narrow, yet exact lanes of information processing between sensing and cognition. Elements E and F depict recursive and circular nature of all elements, A-F. Element G depicts culmination of all elements and their outcomes, with social difference subsequently feeding back into the model.

The core aspects of this theory are summarized in the chapter that follows.

Insights into the Theory of Sensory Cognitive Difference

Based on this theory, the construct of intelligence and that of wisdom or discernment are not equal, at least from the perspective of ASD individuals.

Within discernment, those with autism suggest that a harmony of ideas is needed, not a model of consensus, if we wish to reach a deeper and more meaningful understanding. I believe this calls for more openness and inclusivity for all as a first step in understanding and supporting those with ASD.

Sensory processing differences, likened to an eight lane super-highway (with those who are neurotypical presumably working from a single or possibly a two-lane highway of sensory input), have caused pain, anxiety, fatigue, and perhaps even trauma for individuals with ASD to varying degrees. Within this analogy, both hyper- and hypo- responding are the result.

Additional consideration and understanding for those with autism to address sensory dysregulation based on sounds, lights, touch, texture, taste, and smell are all worthy of consideration for their effects on energy, focus, memory, cognition, and ultimately, sustainability.

At least for those who contributed to this work, there exists an extreme pattern of responding to the sensory sensation of sound that was either highly hyper-sensitive (i.e., physical pain in the ears) or is remarkably hypo-sensitive (does not hear emergency warning systems), and these seem to align closely with either the visual or the verbal learning style pattern, respectively. Since I first heard this from the participants in the study, I have added formal testing to my practice to assess individuals with autism for their auditory discrimination skills. I have yet to test a single person with autism that doesn't have exceptionally good hearing contrasted against very poor speech-sound discrimination skills.

In addition to sound sensitivity, it appears that the "verbal facts people," who are possibly less sensitive to sound (although quite hypo-sensitive in some cases), are able to perform better academically. To me, this suggests that addressing sound is a critical element for performance in the classroom.

Recall that those who were sensitive to sound in this work (the visual learners) were similarly sensitive to certain lights. Fluorescent and LED lights were particularly offensive, causing headaches and, over time, significant performance degradation. While some had light sensitivity, a similar, extreme pattern of hypo-responding was reported in several cases where attention to lights was almost non-existent. As was true in the above instance, those with hypo-responding experienced fewer problems in school and had less sensory effects in the workplace. This will also require attention in schools and in the workplace.

Issues with touch and texture were reported by more than half of the respondents in the study, with some of them experiencing pain or alternate site sensation when touched lightly. Those who felt the sensation in a place other than where they were touched described needing to learn how to process touch from childhood, which ultimately has allowed them to be able to manage touch or even enjoy being touched as adults. Touch is therefore an important topic to consider when working with children on the spectrum.

About half of the study's participants reported issues with tactile sensations pertaining to food, with two of them still being quite limited by what they could eat. Several also disclosed the need to wear certain fabrics or textures of clothing, although I wondered how many of them as adults instinctively choose clothing by their fabric and therefore didn't report, or even recognize a problem with skin sensitivity. No specific pattern of learning style difference seemed to be associated with these areas of sensory difference, although tastes and smells were related to energy levels for those in the study, with the volunteers reporting being able to handle strong tastes or smells better when rested. Others reported appreciating or even enjoying heightened olfaction and taste sensations. Again, sensitivity in these areas did not seem to be aligned with either learning style or other areas of hyper- or hypo-responding; in other words, one could be highly sensitive to sounds or lights, but then have little to no awareness of, or heightened reactions to, strong smells or tastes or tactile sensations. For these reasons, respecting clothing preferences and food choices to the degree possible is probably best for those with ASD.

Apparently, sensory processing differences can also result in challenges with coordination for some with ASD. Discussions about sensory difference suggest that in states of extreme sensory overload, complete impairment of certain motor functions might be possible, with motor shut-downs contributing to issues with safety. These clearly need to be taken into account in all discussions that pertain to the health and safety of these children.

As the topic of difference emerged, there appeared to be considerable diversity amongst those with ASD, and at least two very strong style differences contrasted the "visual/sensory people" and the "verbal facts people." These differences in learning style for those with ASD seem to occur irrespective of and unrelated to the autism or Asperger diagnosis. While it appears on the surface that more individuals with ASD are visual and/or sensorial in their learning style, this distinction is an important one to make, because being either a "visual/sensory person" or a "verbal facts person" appears to have significant implications for a number of other important variables.

For those ASD individuals who are much "lower functioning" or non-vocal, as is assumed by many in the autism community, it should be considered possible that some environmental injury has occurred alongside genetic ASD. This means that assuming potential while also considering possible causes and treatments for the things that are injuring those with autism is critical to support those most affected by their autism.

Strong, interest-based, hyper-focusing ability for the singular, contrasted by an inability to focus on the broad or general seems to exist for individuals with ASD. Accordingly, this leads to difficulties with multitasking but allows for extreme focus, which ultimately facilitates the ability to see the big picture once enough small pieces are put into place. This information should certainly become a part of any teacher training program geared towards teaching those with autism.

One's singularity of focus is driven first and foremost by interests; followed by focus that is directed towards things that are novel, odd, or disturbing. Given the effort required to filter the sensory environment, ASD interests became one of the primary bases for filtering. For this reason, interest-based learning should be an important part of educational programming for these individuals.

I believe that many individuals with autism experience a literal inability to focus on that which isn't interesting. This results in a focus that is not general in nature, but instead is usually very specific and built upon the particular (interest-based concepts). This appears to account for at least some of the cognitive differences reported for individuals with ASD, and as a result, focusing on and attending to patterns has evolved as a strength. Finding ways to use this strength to the benefit of the individual seems to make sense.

Although expected, a learning-style pattern (visual versus verbal) was not specifically identified. Even for ASD individuals who are "verbal facts people," interests and focus for visual patterns often are more well-developed; the "verbal facts people" do seem to have a stronger ability to focus and discern rhythms, sounds, and/or language-based patterns, however.

Similar in its evolution, cognitive difference also seems to develop out of excellent long-term memory that is usually very specific and detailed, although not very general, for individuals with ASD. With poor short-term memory, the individuals who contributed to this work reported experiencing memory in a way that is well beyond that of most neurotypical people for the specific, although reports suggest that memory usually occurs within what several described as a narrow window of observation that is nearly perfect in detail. As was true for focus, memory differences need to be understood and used to help educate those with ASD.

The volunteers for this work hypothesized that even for the "verbal facts people," visual memory is especially sophisticated in most people with ASD. Some individuals with ASD appear to have even developed the ability to see and remember freeze-frame photographs for particular events or social sequences, which reportedly can then be stopped or replayed at various speeds. This interesting trend has some incredibly useful benefits and could be developed to help those with ASD compensate for poorer skill development in other areas.

Because of different experiences, and perhaps even areas of specific strength within neurodiversity for memory and visual perception, there appears to be a tendency for those with ASD to be able to apply these skills and attributes to understanding the metaphysical and high-level quantum physics. These skills, too, should be encouraged.

Other perspectives within memory suggest that for some, memories can be easily compartmentalized, although this might lead to aspects of difficulty with object-permanence, especially for those who were often in a new location for work. This needs to be more thoroughly explored and understood for its relationship to reality-checking and object-permanence in young or severely affected children with ASD.

While learning style seemed to play out in the other categories, surprisingly, both the verbal and the visual learners in this study seemed to have strong visual memory, although the "verbal facts people" also remembered everything that was said in addition to the other visual and sensory memories they had. Knowing how memories are stored and retrieved for those with ASD is an extremely valuable tool in helping them learn.

Some ASD individuals who are exceptionally visual seem to also have strong, three-dimensional spatial memory as well (although this seems quite the opposite for the "verbal facts" group). The role that spatial reasoning plays in vocational success seems to tie closely to Temple Grandin's statements earlier about untapped potential for those with ASD in the fields of STEM.

Memory also seemed to play a significant role in compensation of skill deficits, particularly in areas of multi-tasking and executive functioning, although those in the study reported that their memories were "filled with holes." Much more understanding about memory as a strength-based attribute is needed for those with ASD.

Cognitive differences, particularly within the seeing or sensing of patterns, finding or recognizing anomalies, attending to details, and/or re-creating and imagining the big picture from the assemblage of parts, appear to be the most remarkable areas of cognitive, strength-based difference for people with ASD. These align closely to aptitude in the STEM fields and should be capitalized on for their contribution to vocational success for those with ASD.

Cognitive differences result in what those in this work described as "slowed processing speed and challenges with the articulation of idea for conversational output." In other words, people with ASD often require extra time to process. So, we should give them extra time to process without reservation or judgment.

In line with being able to easily see the big picture, the individuals who contributed to this work indicated how new learning required them to learn from the specific instance to the general until the big picture could be created. From there, mapping a path and detailing the steps to get from point A to point B in tasks were reported as challenges—although having a narrowed focus and the ability to pay attention to the singular helped to some degree once an organizational list was created. These are all valuable insights to help those with ASD learn and reach their full potentials.

Given what appears to be a very different manifestation of cognition for individuals with ASD, most of the affected feel riddled with areas of significant cognitive aptitude amidst debilitating deficits. Cognitive differences are blamed for poor performance, slowed responding, and challenges in communication as the inherently linear nature of language makes speaking hard, even for the "verbal facts people." Understanding the deep impact of asynchronous development for those with ASD will be an important aspect in helping them understand their autism and feel whole.

Interpreted within the tradition of the cyclical and recursive nature of all our mental abilities as described by Glass & Holyoak, the participants who contributed to this work articulated how their sensory differences take everything in but are best narrowed down by specific bands of interest and remembered within highly detailed and specific memories. This leads those with ASD to very different places in their thinking. For many with ASD, this evolution of cognitive skill difference does not line up with standardized assessments of intelligence or performance ability, and this has caused most to feel like the existing systems of evaluation are rigged against them. It is reasonable to assume that standardized tests don't do their job for this group.

With an inability to prove their intelligence, individuals with ASD have arrived at a variety of opinions about interpreting intellectual abilities for those who are more impaired in their verbal skills or delayed in motor demonstration abilities. ASD individuals are calling for open discussions about the possibility of multiple and alternative forms of visual or sensory difference within aspects of cognitive performance that are not reliant on fast-responding or verbal output.

To give clarity to cognitive difference in ASD, according to those who contributed to this work it seems that a picture is worth a thousand words. But, because so many words are required to relay a full-blown sensory experience, these experiences become simply too complex to put into language.

This leads those with ASD to view processing within traditional verbal communication systems as unnecessarily linear. As such, visual communication systems could be explored for this population.

Given differences between cognitive strengths and weaknesses between neurotypical individuals and those with ASD, there seems to be valid indicators to support alternative forms of cognition for some individuals with ASD. Perhaps it is time to reopen discussions about what cognition actually is.

As what almost all in this study felt was their primary feature of disability, speaking the ideas that were in their heads, the topic of speculation opened to suggest that some non-vocal members of the ASD community (often deemed to be "low-functioning"), might in fact experience an even more extreme difference in cognition, memory, focus, and sensory responding that ultimately leads to a state of hyper-visualizing which competes for resources at the expense of language and motor skills. In addition to rethinking cognition, I feel "low-functioning" autism must also be rethought entirely.

With ties to all of the other points listed above, it was suggested that the natures of cognition, memory difference, focus, and sensory difference are simply too expansive to articulate outside of discussions with those who are not on the spectrum. This calls for inclusion of those with autism in all discussions about autism.

Furthermore, continuous processing is exhausting from a cognitive energy standpoint, and individuals with ASD must work very hard to conserve their cognitive resources for use in necessary tasks. For many with autism, a part-time schedule should be equated with a full-time workload.

With little surprise, the adults who contributed to the study and subsequently to this book identified with a number of challenges in processing social information. For the first of these, remarkable childhood histories have led at least some with ASD to view social interaction from a position of safety and self-preservation. For this reason, those with autism need to be more carefully protected from social assaults (by the both their peers and the adults in their lives).

For people with ASD, social communication issues are part and parcel to the majority of the challenges faced in the social arena. Communication difficulties in ASD include issues with processing verbal communication in noise, timing responses, knowing when and how to enter or exit a conversation, cognitively tracking the conversation, and sharing interests. These social communication skills could be targeted for instruction within social programs and social skills classes.

Many people with ASD feel that the majority of social interactions they are accused of being bad at are riddled with inauthenticity and small-talk. Social challenge is described as *a difference*, but certainly not *the primary difference* in ASD. All participants in this study described some challenges with reading and interpreting nonverbal cues. While some of the social differences in autism should be addressed, it seems that we "neurotypicals" could also learn a lot about social ethics from those who have autism.

Strategies to address social differences by those in the study include reading people as either good or bad, associating mostly with good people or with people who are friends, and coping with social difference—particularly in unfamiliar social arenas—by choosing varying degrees of self-isolation. Final thoughts were shared tying the social to cognitive difference for relationship to the use of energy and cost-versus-benefit value of socializing. Perhaps having some time away from peers to regroup and build energy is an important part of helping someone with ASD.

With these main ideas and the relationships between them established, I arrived at the conclusion that differences in sensory processing, focus, memory, and cognitive processing all crossed, interacted, and co-mingled to explain a very different form of sensory-cognitive evolution for individuals with ASD. This results ultimately in thinking and social interaction differences. From this conclusion, the theory of sensory-cognitive difference emerged as a more complete and in-depth understanding about how the relationships between intelligence, cognition, and sensory processing might be explained for those with ASD.

CHAPTER NINE

Where Do We Go from Here?

To begin this section, I would like to open with a question, "Is being on the spectrum worse than not being on the spectrum, especially for those who are 'high-functioning?'" Based on what I have learned in my career and from the findings of this study, I have come to believe that, as educators and mental health professionals, we need to be asking ourselves if we are doing the best we can for those with ASD to raise them up into healthy, happy adults who have the skills, self-knowledge, and resources to become well-adjusted contributing members of the future world.

In thinking about this question for myself, I can't seriously say I have an answer, especially for the children I have worked with who are diagnosed to be on the spectrum of autism. But I can say that it is clear to me, especially having conducted this study, that it is high time we start doing things in a dramatically different way for today's youth with ASD. Because right now, driving them through a deficit-based system that only identifies and strives to remediate what they can't do in an effort to normalize them is tantamount to losing them.

We see these youngsters in our classrooms, in the main-stream media, and even within our own families; but for those with ASD, I believe that we still just don't understand enough about autism to know what to do differently. Therefore, with a hope that is perhaps too naïve and too optimistic, I would like to put forth the alternative theory of sensory-cognitive difference to begin to more fully understand, implement, and carry out how we address the needs (both strengths and deficits) for individuals diagnosed with ASD.

First and foremost, because I believe that nothing can or ever will change without increased knowledge and understanding. I think that the words of those with ASD, as reported throughout this book, offer some of the most valuable contributions ever spoken about ASD. I think these words fill gaps that have existed in our understanding about autism since autism was first introduced. This work opens broad topics for discussion on intelligence, cognition, and sensory processing in ASD, and in so doing, provides insight and wisdom from those affected. The work also adds this: important as socialization might seem to the rest of us, social difference isn't necessarily that important to those with autism. So, what do we do with all this new information? The following sections detail my thoughts about moving forward.

Thoughts about the Rise of the Autism Diagnosis

While the cause of autism is still widely disputed, the numbers of individuals diagnosed is clearly on the rise. But, according to several of the participants who contributed to my study, "injury" in what should otherwise be considered a neurodiverse or different form of development for those with autism might actually be the cause for the increasing numbers. In other words, the autism community believes that autism itself is a normal, albeit neurodiverse, aspect within the general population, and these individuals should not be viewed as disabled but instead as different. However, for those who are more severe, the notion of *injury in autism* applies and, therefore, needs to be addressed.

For this reason, continued research on both environmental and epigenetic causality must continue. However, this should be done within the idea that perhaps not all autism should be viewed through a lens of disability, but instead should be seen from the standpoint of happy, healthy functioning of the neurodiverse individual.

Effects on Learning and Socialization

Second, the conditions of autism might have a significant and negative effect on socialization and learning, especially when viewed through the lens of what is neurotypical. Based on what individuals in these works had to say, it is possible that the over-emphasis on what is socially normal or on what is normal in learning might overlook some valuable insights from those with ASD about what should be considered as normal for both socializing and learning in ASD. Those who contributed to this work reported that shallow conversations with inauthentic people are simply not worth the cost. Additionally, it seems that a different form of social identity development might relate to key social differences in ASD. Furthermore, for those with ASD, it seems possible the construct of learning might be long overdue for an overhaul to include definitions of learning within the interest-based focus, specific memory systems, and cognitive differences that seem to have evolved within the conditions of autism.

Intellectual Disability in Autism

Regarding the topic of intellectual disability, for those who weighed in, especially those who self-aligned with being "very visual," it seems possible that IQ scores are not at all accurate in ASD. Two of the participants in the research had completed doctoral level studies and yet had been tested as children with IQ scores near the intellectually disabled range. Clearly, the construct of intelligence—at least for those with ASD—might be worthy of another look. Furthermore, assumptions about prevailing intellectual disability might merely be reflecting the side-effects of an outdated construct of intelligence for those with ASD.

Existing Cognitive Theories

A number of unique cognitive difference theories have attempted to explain autism over the years, though none yet appear to be universal. However, based on my findings, the theories of mind blindness, executive functioning, weak central coherence, and hyper-systemizing all seem to hold pieces of the equation. Like strings on a guitar, I see the addition of the theory of sensory-cognitive difference as a needed component to round out the explanation of autism for a more harmonious big picture. Unlike previous research, my study focused specifically on strengths and first-person accounts, and this led to a new starting point in the discovery of a very different and unique form of sensory processing. Within this theory, sensory information for those with ASD is filtered by interest-based observation and remembered through detail and specifics within a narrow but perfect window that evolves into a different form of cognition. This culminates in social difference and is cycled back into sensory perception difference. This new theory has parts of all of the existing theories embedded within it at different stages, but I believe that because no one has ever looked at autism for what it actually is from the perspective of those diagnosed, we have missed the bigger picture about ASD.

The Extreme Nature of Sensory Difference

Clearly, within this proposed harmony of models, there is universal agreement that sensory processing difference underlies the conditions of autism. However, based on the findings of my work, it appears that what has been lacking is an understanding of the extreme nature of difference that those with ASD experience. Moreover, it is still very unclear how sensory processing difference impacts cognitive evolution within an individual. According to the members of my research group, that difference is so great that it cannot be explained in words. In turn, this seems to have prevented clarity about what sensory difference actually is or how it plays out in focus and the development of memory within the learning environment. With sensory difference confirmed, much more research is needed on how to adapt the environment to meet the needs of the individual, instead of the other way around.

Although not clearly a finding of this study, in talking with the volunteers and numerous private clients about their sensory difference, I have learned that sensory differences have even resulted in trauma in some cases. For this reason, I think additional research in the area of sensory trauma and its effects on cognitive development seems like a worthy cause, especially in attempts to address the needs of those affected individuals who are severely impaired or for those who seem to be in constant pain.

Hyper- and Hypo-Responding

Within the sensory processing research, either hypo-sensitivity or hyper-sensitivity are heavily reported. With little to explain these or tie them to any kind of meaningful pattern of responding, using this study as a starting point, more research could be done to determine if there is, indeed, a higher pattern of hypo-responding in those who are inherently the "verbal facts people" and, similarly, a more extreme pattern of hyper-responding for those who are more visual or sensorial in their inherent learning-style make-up.

The Need to Address Sensory Differences First

Within the proposed strength-based sensory-cognitive theory of difference that came out of my research, I envision that more emphasis will need to be given to what those with ASD do differently and to what they can do well. Trying to teach a child math facts or how to write their letters makes little sense during periods where the child is so sensorially overwhelmed that they feel as if their very life depends on attaining some change in the sensory environment. Based on the reports from the study, it appears that those with ASD should never be forced into settings where noise is painful for them; nor should they have to exist and function under fluorescent or LED lights. Attention to touch and texture must include the possibility that touch is painful or confusing and should, therefore, be avoided. Furthermore, the sensory support diet of any individual with ASD should take into account such things as clothing preferences and the ability to be in a setting that isn't confounded by strong smells. Those with ASD should never be forced to eat foods that don't agree with their palate. As stated by so many ASD individuals I have known through the years, until those with ASD understand their sensory processing systems and feel safe, they won't be able to think or learn.

Cognitive Difference

To address cognitive differences, it appears that research and development is needed on a teaching method that is particular to the skills of: (a) hyper-focusing on the interest-based singular; (b) remembering with acute clarity the details within the narrow; (c) seeing and/or creating the big picture; (d) recognizing patterns, rhythms, and anomalies; and (e) processing on a different time clock for intuitive solutions to problems. This will require a shift in teaching those with ASD to do much more than ABA therapy for inclusion in the classroom. By expanding research into the areas of attention, focus, cognitive difference, and processing speed, new research-driven teaching practices could ultimately evolve. In addition to supporting and teaching sensory awareness, educators in both K-12 programs and in higher education will need to be taught how to truly understand and address cognitive differences for those with ASD, which will require autism-specific training programs that specialize in preparing educators to be able to meet the cognitive difference needs for individuals with ASD.

Increased support and training in self-advocacy as well as improved legal supports will also be required for change to occur in the workplace. Given what is now known in the fields of behaviorism, cognitive learning theory, the cognitive neurosciences, and sensory processing theory, the only universally accepted and research-approved therapies for the treatment of ASD continue to be found within the traditions of behaviorism. This needs to change. More specifically, based on the findings from my research, it appears that the adults with ASD who have been professionally successful (i.e., able to support themselves and live independently) all found a way to work through their sensory challenges and find employment within an area of strength, interest, or passion. However, for those stuck in menial jobs or jobs well below their training, sensory issues and a lack of vocational support were cited as reasons for not being professionally successful. To address needs effectively, both educational and vocational training must first address sensory issues by helping those with ASD learn to manage their differences, advocate for them, and seek reasonable accommodations in the workplace. As indicated by some in this study, both special education and civil liberty laws need to more fully recognize and mandate change for those with ASD who cannot function due to their sensory differences within the existing definitions of "reasonable accommodation." Once sensory issues have been addressed, formal identification of strengths, teaching toward those strengths, and support for the alignment of strength-based job placement with training in the workplace is needed.

Alignment and Difference to Neuro-Diversity Theory

Given the complex nature of the proposed theory of sensory-cognitive difference, research in the field of neurobiology should take a hint from the neurodiversity movement. New research should pursue more strength- and difference-based world views on the spectrum of autism.

Very much in line with the recent neurodiversity theory being forwarded by many of those with ASD, the theory of sensory-cognitive difference, as proposed, gives specificity to a different form of epigenetic evolution for those with ASD. However, unlike the neurodiversity theory, this theory also recognized the possibility that environmental assault in recent decades might also have injured many ASD individuals. Therefore, rather than accept all forms of autism as part of the normal neurodiverse continuum, this theory, as proposed by some of the respondents within, recommends continued research and intervention (especially within the fields of medicine and occupational therapy) to support and alleviate the distress of those who might be otherwise on a different neurodiverse path.

CHAPTER NINE

Challenging Assumptions and the Implication in Doing So

From its outset, my research aimed to address gaps in the evidence-based literature by exploring the topics of intelligence, cognition, and sensory processing for the purpose of establishing a theory that could effectively challenge existing assumptions and provide alternative recommendations for those with ASD. Therefore, to give further clarity and depth to the proposed theory of sensory-cognitive difference, the following discussion and recommendations are provided for the purposes of more completely explaining the theory while challenging assumptions and filling gaps.

Definitions of Autism

The first assumption I challenge within this theory is that a universally agreed-upon definition of autism exists. Within the proposed theory, it is clear to me that the conditions of autism are, indeed, on a continuum, although the learning styles of "verbal facts people" versus those who are "visual/sensory people" appear distinct. These do not, in my mind, constitute the primary differences first articulated between Kanner and Asperger, and they are certainly are not reflected within the diagnoses of autism or Asperger's syndrome. Instead, I see them as a different starting base for learning that is probably genetic. My theory, therefore, proposes that there was no difference between the cases of Kanner and Asperger (recall that I read some of the original case studies in preparation for this study), but that the primary differences we see across the continuum of functioning as "high" or "low" are, instead, differences of ability for managing sensory differences and for vocalization. I believe that it is entirely possible that for those we are now describing as "low-functioning" or nonverbal, these individuals might simply be too specialized within the visual and sensory domains for *vocalization* and efficient motor planning (based on opinions of three of the participants in this study who are also parents to "lower-functioning" children). For this reason, much more needs to be done to understand sensory and learning style differences for individuals across the entire autism spectrum.

The Prevalence of Intellectual Disability in Autism Spectrum Disorder

The second, and perhaps the most problematic, assumption I would like to challenge is that intellectual disability continues to be assumed for individuals across the autism spectrum. In line with the above point and within the proposed theory of sensory-cognitive difference's position that sensory and cognitive development have evolved together into a very different form of intelligence, I believe that for those with ASD, intelligence might actually exist outside of the definitions and limits that have been placed on it by Spearman and others. Moreover, for those with ASD, intelligence is something much more diverse and complex than we who are neurotypical can even imagine. Thus, we should all use our basic nature of discernment instead of some standardized score or IQ prediction to ascertain intelligence for those with ASD. In all cases, the presumption of cognitive competence must precede any discussions about intelligence or its measurement for those diagnosed with an autism spectrum disorder. Therefore, at present, I think we lack the instruments to measure it consistently. Because our existing measures fail to include those things that are specialized in ASD within the core construct of intelligence, I think that intelligence and, likely, performance in ASD cannot be accurately measured. With the added problem that most testing environments are likely not adapted to the basic sensory needs of individuals with ASD, those who are most affected possibly can't even think while being tested. It is my recommendation that we "throw out the baby with the bathwater" as it pertains to assessment for those with ASD and rely, instead, on our basic nature of discernment to start over and rethink about intelligence in ASD.

In my career, I have heard at least 100 times that a particular child is "just so smart, but his test scores are very low," and yet, these same insightful educators who picked up on high ability are still forced to rely more on the scores than on their instincts, given special education requirements. In all cases, a presumption of cognitive competence needs to be assumed for those with ASD until we have the ability to assess those with ASD for their unique abilities and differences. I do believe that there are differences in intelligence across the spectrum and that these are likely to be at least as extreme as in the NT population, but until we understand them, we will be unable to sort intellectual disability from giftedness. I also believe that what we now constitute as intelligence might actually fall away completely once we begin to more fully understand sensory and cognitive difference for those with ASD. For all these reasons, I call for the abandonment of formal assessment data used in placement decision-making for all individuals with ASD who score below eighty on formal IQ tests. For these individuals, I recommend that instead of IQ-achievement data, first-person reports by those familiar with the individual be used to develop individualized learning plans to address both strengths and needs.

Views on the Evolution of Behavior and Cognition

In line with the previous discussion, I also challenge developmental worldviews on the evolution of behavior and cognition for their ability to capture cognitive abilities and differences for those with ASD. Using the idea that cognition should include all our mental abilities, I propose that the fields of behaviorism, cognitive learning theory, and even neurobiology stop specifically comparing those with autism to those who are "developmentally normal." Autism does not follow a "normal" development path. These fields should instead focus on what is different and what could be developed out of these differences. More specifically, the primarily language-based tasks of short-term verbal memory and spoken or written recall that have historically been heavily associated with learning and, thus, vocational outcomes may no longer predict vocational fields in the future as they have in the past, especially for those with ASD. Therefore, I believe we, as a society, must consider new and alternative methods of learning and performance for our economic sustainability in general—and more specifically, for those with the special talents of autism. It is clear to me that our current educational trajectory, especially for the millions of children with autism and sensory-cognitive differences, is not adequately preparing these individuals for careers in the STEM fields where they are most likely to find success. With those with ASD as the largest growing career sector in the world, I believe it is possible that a shift in education to focus on preparing students for entry into STEM is what both the massive numbers of those with ASD and the job market of 2020 will require. This is not to say that all individuals with ASD should be forced into the STEM fields, but instead, the door should be opened for them to try if they feel interested and inclined to do so, and educational training programs should align closely with that mission.

Views on Sensory Difference

An additional problematic assumption that I believe I challenge within this work is the assumption that the way humans perceive and process sensory information from the external world is the same for everyone. In this assumption, I referred to the original works of Jean Ayres. Now more than ever, with the voices of the participants with me in this research, I would like to reiterate my belief that the real value of Ayres' sensory integration theory was that it scratched the surface of understanding how truly complex, pervasive, and multi-dimensional the effects of sensory processing are for all levels of processing and individual cognitive evolution. With the sensory systems now recognized for their involvement, at nearly all levels of cognitive processing, it is no wonder that the demonstration of intellectual ability or learning and performance seem to be dramatically affected by sensory processing difference. Within this finding, I recommend that the field of sensory processing theory be re-opened and re-examined for its relationship to the very different evolution of sensory processing that seems to have occurred for those with ASD.

Views on What is Normal

Similar to the argument above and of paramount consideration within this research is the final question I posed in the opening of this summary, "Is autism, especially in its 'higher forms' of functioning, somehow worse than being normal?" More specifically, I am asking, "Should everyone be normal?" Within the existing developmental world-view, those with ASD are dissected and classified for their deficits, while my work suggests that a much more *whole-istic*, strength-based view will undoubtedly reveal both challenges and strengths that are normal for those with ASD. Within this, a much broader definition of "normal" must evolve, and the arrogance of trying to make everyone alike must be abandoned. To do this, teacher training and educational programming must ultimately move away from discussions about bringing every child up to some developmental normal and, instead, expand into broader discussions and deeper understanding about diversity and the need for inclusive, strength-based identification and talent development.

On Being Whole

Through advances in neurobiology, researchers continue to claim to be able to see visible differences in the brains of those with ASD. But without the ability to analyze these differences within their broader, systematic global functioning as a *whole system*, a large number of disconnected brain differences continue to be explored as *abnormalities*. Within my proposed theory of sensory-cognitive difference, I suggest that, of course, those with ASD will have differences in their brains. In fact, with such significant sensory and cognitive differences, the reverse would be impossible to imagine. But I would like to propose the idea that until we consider those with ASD against themselves (i.e., gather data about what is normal in autism), there will never be a situation in which we can determine what is normal or abnormal for those with ASD. Interpreted through the lens of the combined theories of causation that draw both from epigenetics and the environment (namely, toxic loading theories that damage those with ASD), I believe that we cannot look at ASD as a dissected variant of "normal" because in so doing, we miss the critical step of finding and stopping what is damaging some ASD kids to more severe levels. It is, therefore, time that we start looking at those with ASD from a fresh, *whole-person* perspective.

Future Research

Given the rich and insightful voice of several highly self-aware participants who have lived with and interacted within autism communities for most of their lives, I feel comfortable forwarding their thoughts to inform and recommend future research. Based on the thoughts of those in this inquiry, the following recommendations for future research seem logical.

It appears that the rise in autism likely has both a genetic and an "environmental injury" component. Furthermore, while this book specifically excluded the body of research I considered for the study within the field of neuroscience for the causality of autism, I have within my research come to the conclusion that while many brain-based differences are present in ASD (as is probably true for any other neurodiverse group that is similarly dissected), autism is most likely the result of several complex genetic traits (or to use a term from my field, learning style differences) that are particularly keen to the world and also especially susceptible to damage from toxic load from the environment. I believe these two variables will eventually converge and tie neuro-modulation and sensory processing differences to cognitive evolution that is outside of traditional definitions of adaptation and functioning. For this reason, ongoing research into causality that includes both epigenetics and environmental loading theories seems appropriate.

While issues with socialization are present in autism, it is recommended that these be researched for their effects on the individual with ASD, instead of from the perspective comparing NT and ASD groups or training ASD groups to act "normally." Research on which social skills to teach and how to teach social skills should be directed by those with the condition. In some areas, I believe NTs have a lot to learn about social interaction from those with ASD.

On the research topics of intellectual disability, existing measures do not tap the potentials of those with ASD due to challenges with motor planning, processing speed, and difficulty communicating. These are furthered hampered by sensory issues such as fluorescent lights or competing background noises in most school-testing environments. As such, new studies that re-think intelligence, that attempt to find ways to truly capture learning styles and strengths, and that explore testing methods that are capable of allowing those with ASD to truly demonstrate their unique skill sets seem important. Until testing for those with ASD can change dramatically, however, it appears that the use of existing assessment tools might be less valid than the clinical reports of those who work closely with these individuals. In other words, estimates about intelligence might need to be assumed from those who see the gifts. I believe that the individuals who contributed to my study and this book seriously question the construct of intelligence, because it doesn't specifically include some the key things they believe should be included within any definition of intelligence. Until further tools have been developed to re-open discussions about actual intelligence in autism, the use of existing tools to measure or "prove" intelligence in autism needs to be replaced with observation and the reports of those who know these children well.

New discussions about intelligence in autism will require considerable research on the topic of different forms of intelligence in autism.

Visual languages and visual communication tools for their usefulness with non-vocal individuals were recommended by one of the participants as a method that might be able to reach some of those who appear "low-functioning."

As traditional definitions of learning are also negatively affected by ASD, based on the comments made by those in this book, it appears that much more insight is needed surrounding the topics of interest-based focus and long-term memory for their applications to learning and performance.

Given that this study proposed an alternate theory about the sensory and cognitive differences of those with ASD, much more will need to be done to verify or refute the theory of sensory-cognitive difference beyond this group to the broader autism spectrum.

To do this, it appears that the topic of sensory processing difference needs to be seriously re-considered for those with ASD, especially within its relationship to cognition. Specific areas to explore related to this topic include: (a) the extreme states that hyper- and hypo-responding can take; (b) the role of sound sensitivity and auditory discrimination in cognition and learning; (c) the effects of lighting on energy and attention; and (d) the possibility of a significant learning style difference between the "verbal facts people" and those who are highly visual for their difference in thinking and sensory responding.

More challenging still, I think it is time for new discussions to emerge on the topic of cognition in autism. What is clear to me is that a very different form of cognition might be present in autism, but in spite of over 800,000 clinical studies to explore other aspects, very few have taken the time to ask those with autism about how they think. To my knowledge, no studies have fully captured the strength-based abilities in cognition that I have seen in the ASD individuals that I have known throughout my life. I think that because much of the research on cognition has focused heavily on what those with ASD can't do—or more specifically, what they can or can't do compared to NTs—the body of research on autism has failed to witness the emergence of *whole* individuals with very specific strengths that I'm not sure exist anywhere else within the general population. Based on what I have learned, specific areas to consider include the following: (a) the strength-based skills of hyper-focusing; (b) interest-based learning; (c) long-term, sensory-based memory; (d) creating or envisioning the big picture; (e) recognizing patterns, rhythms, and anomalies; and (f) processing speed as it relates to intuitive thinking, problem solving, and communicating. In addition, more understanding is needed within the topic of communication as so many of these individuals are clearly highly verbal, but struggle with vocalization.

Once the cognitive abilities of those with ASD are better understood, then research on how to teach to these must follow. It is my opinion that the body of research geared towards finding new ways to "fix deficits" or "normalize" those with ASD is fully saturated. However, learning more about the sensory-cognitive continuum in ASD should result in a better understanding of strengths and needs. In turn, this will improve understanding and inform teaching toward better educational programming for those with ASD.

I think more research is also needed to understand the actual variables that have helped adults with autism find success in the workplace. Too many children and youth today have no future until the systems that are in place can teach them what is needed to overcome their hurdles and find a use for their strengths. Within this, I believe much more needs to be done to adapt educational systems for both school-age kids with ASD and for young adults who have aged out of public-school programs to understand and apply their strengths to usable skills.

Finally, I think it is certainly time for research and discussion about what those with ASD can do, within a whole-person perspective, instead of what they can't do when compared to the developmental "normal." This means that a shift away from reductionist and developmental world views might be long overdue.

CHAPTER TEN

Endings and Beginnings

Thirty years ago, at the beginning of my career, I met two young men that forever changed my life. The first of these was Timmy. He was four years old, diagnosed with autism, and knew every adult team member (approximately forty-five people) by their license plate number.

I had just landed my first job in the field of autism and I was working at the center where Timmy went to preschool. This school was particularly well known for its expertise in serving those with autism and approximately 100 children between the ages two to six attended from all over the United States.

I remember on my very first day, during a new teacher orientation, I was told that all the children at the center (including Timmy), in spite of whether or not they could speak, would never graduate from high school, go to college, live independently, or be able to productively contribute to their society; none would have true friendships, none would marry, and none would have children of their own as autism was a genetic disease.

Presented to me as something of a noble calling, I was told that my primary responsibility in this position was to help these kids learn how to act appropriately, fit in, and as much as possible, attend school and learn to model the normal behaviors of their peers. When I asked about Timmy's ability to identify people by their license plates (something I had witnessed when I first toured the school), a prim woman in a tan suit (who will forever be etched into my memory holding a blue clipboard and a hand-held counter clicker) firmly told me that while some of these kids "might seem" to have certain advanced abilities, these were not to be viewed as usable skills and should instead be referred to as "splinter skills."

When I attempted to interject an argument on Timmy's behalf, she firmly said, "No, Marlo, Timmy's ability in this area will never amount to anything useful and we need to be very careful to not let these little things we see give us false hope. Timmy has autism, which is a very severe and disabling lifelong developmental disability."

I have often marveled about all the people we meet in our lives and the very few that stand out vividly in our long-term memories, but for me, the second boy that I still think about often is Sam. After my time working with young children, with supervisors who deemed me qualified to call myself a certified behavior therapist, I helped a colleague from the center where I had worked with Timmy to take on the most cognitively impaired and "lowest functioning" six young adult members of the Utah State Hospital system. These young men were making their transition to group homes as the state was closing all its state-run facilities. As a newly minted behavior therapist, I had been assigned to a home with overnight and weekend responsibilities (which were not as desirable for those of us who had completed the full course of behavior training).

My position called upon its staff to help the residents prepare, eat, and clean up their meals; complete cleaning and house-work jobs; then we assisted the young men with evening leisure activities. This included things like playing board games, going to the local recreation center, taking a walk at the park, or having dessert at a nearby frozen yogurt shop. We sometimes even participated in social outings with other group homes. Our days at work concluded with helping the residents take their evening showers, setting out the laundry, various rituals and bedtime routines, and the dispensing of medications. Then it was "lights out" and we were left in quiet to study or watch television until the morning shift came on duty.

The young men in our home included a man who was sweet and calm, until he wasn't—his arm regularly in a cast because he had routinely broken it in fits of rage; a stripper who, whenever in public, would elope and take off all of his clothes, hands flapping and masturbating as he ran; a teenage boy who ate almost everything (the technical term for this is pica) including his clothing, trash, and at times, even feces; an older man (nearly thirty) who struggled with severe obsessive-compulsive tendencies in addition to his autism that made simple routines (such as taking a shower or doing a load of laundry) a three-hour affair; and Sam, who could become physically aggressive, weighed nearly 300 pounds, and had a tendency to "flirt" with all the girls which included fairly constant attempts to inappropriately touch them on their legs, breasts, or behinds.

Although I will let the reader imagine the more challenging aspects of this job, I can honestly say that in spite of these individuals all being completely non-vocal and exhibiting frightening and sometimes unbelievably difficult behaviors, especially for a young female new to the field, these four out-thought those of us that worked with them on a daily basis; these young men were smart! There was no doubt in my mind that I was living amongst some form of latent genius, even though I had been told that these were the "lowest functioning" of all the residents in the Utah State Hospital.

CHAPTER TEN

The memories that stand out most, though, were our evenings at the swimming pool. In particular, I remember how Sam could hold water in his hands in such a unique way, that when he flipped it into the air, it formed a ball (about the size of a bowling ball). Sam's magical ball of water, when returned to the pool's surface, literally exploded. Sam's therapists tried for hours to repeat the trick and I encourage you to try it, too. Not one of us could figure it out, even with what amounted to a dozen or more hours of practice apiece and perfect modeling of the behavior.

While this might seem like a singular anomaly, across my life's work I have finally come to understand that these magical balls of water for Sam, and that long list of license plate numbers for Timmy, represent the thousands of things that those who live with ASD can do; things which I and others like me cannot.

To this day, I have never stopped wondering what happened to Timmy or Sam or the hundreds of others who have shaped my thinking and even changed the person that I am today. Did Timmy ever find a way to use whatever allowed him to memorize license plates to find a job or live independently? Can Sam still transform water into giant exploding bowling balls at the pool? More importantly, did someone take the time to get to know these individuals, admire them, and see in them what I saw?

Many of those first children from my past would now be in their thirties and forties (I think this makes me officially old). These are now grown men and women and I am pretty sure some of them no longer have living parents to care for them. Also, they are no longer little kids with odd little quirks or talents or unusual "splinter skills." I still wonder, did they find their niche? Do they have jobs? Have they married? Do any of them have children of their own? If so, how is that going for them? Are they happy? Most of all, how have they made their way in an extremely cruel world that is hard even for those of us who do fit in?

While I will probably never know how Timmy's or Sam's stories evolved, like so many others since who have entertained me, fascinated me, and even kept me awake at night with worry, I think I can now imagine a much bigger story and the possibility for a much richer life than the one I was told to expect for these children when I first began working in the field.

I have always kept one foot in the field of gifted education while the other stayed rooted to my passion for autism. I now believe that I have come to see what I think is the shade of grey between giftedness and autism. As such, I'm here to tell you that there is a definitive link between innate cognitive ability and the autism spectrum. I know this will be heavily disputed, so let me be clear, I'm not someone who will tell you that all kids are gifted (although all children are a blessing and have special gifts). I am specifically saying here that I firmly attest to that fact that while cognition isn't the same in autism as it is in our thinking for neurotypicals, in my opinion, a very high level of innate cognitive ability (and thus and a unique and high ability for potential) is present for all individuals with autism.

Furthermore, I have also come to understand that cognition for those with autism can't be properly understood or assessed because it does not fit within our mainstream views about intellect or learning. In fact, I suspect it might even be a type of evolutionary adaptation that has arisen out of what I now believe to be an entirely more sophisticated and advanced system of sensory processing.

On that note, I also believe that within these cognitive differences, individuals with autism have developed entirely different methods to focus and remember. In fact, our measurement tools are so limited that I believe they even prevent us from thinking about cognition as it should be: more fully and completely defined. As such, cognition for those with autism also can't be driven or developed properly within what I feel to be an archaic and outdated mode of modern-day education. Furthermore, cognition and sensory processing can't and shouldn't be dissected, reduced, or understood without a much broader understanding of the possibility of a different and much more complex definition of intelligence. Maybe it is finally time to start rethinking all of our educational, mental health, and even medical models to more fully align with strength-based, person-centered approaches to understanding difference. For this last point, I believe we owe it to those who are neurodiverse to include and consider their input, and we owe it to ourselves to finally get this right. Until we truly learn how to individualize things to meet the unique and diverse needs of all individuals, we are losing the world's most valuable resource: our different minds.

Based on what I learned from my study, I think we have to start down this path by stepping out of our own side of the aisle to consider those who are different as useful and necessary to the survival of our species. This means we really need to start thinking differently about thinking. I know more than anyone that this is a big job. In fact, it might be nearly impossible to do unless your brain has been rattled like mine has. So, since having a brain injury is no fun, I believe the best way to get new insights is to ask neurodiverse people for their thoughts and insights about their own conditions, then listen to what they have to say with an open mind and an open heart.

I've known some individuals who, on paper, have some of the highest measured IQ scores in the world. But even with that as my frame, the most deeply, cognitively brilliant people that I have ever met in an entire career of working and specializing with the gifted have been the ones diagnosed with autism. As such, I would say that my best lessons have always come from the most unusual sources. With work in both of these fields, it is especially clear to me that neurotypicals are not doing such a great job right now of running the world. Perhaps, given a voice, it will be through the most unique, gifted, diverse, and beautifully different-minded individuals that society will finally be able to live, thrive, and create a more sustainable and meaningful existence for us all. Let's all start this journey by stripping away our prejudices and really trying to understand the world from the perspective of someone with autism.

GLOSSARY

Terms and Definitions
Used in this Work

ABILITY. According to the Merriam-Webster collegiate dictionary (2005), ability has three separate definitions that, while similar, account for a difference of agreement about what the term actually means. The first of these suggests that ability is the specific quality or state of being able (physically or mentally) to perform. The second aligns ability with competence and skill; a third definition delineates ability as a natural aptitude or acquired proficiency. Given that this study was particularly interested in both natural aptitudes and the development of acquired performance, specifically considering these for their inherent differences, the term ability in this book was used broadly to include all three definitions, with reservation of the term *latent ability* assigned to those natural aptitudes that are, as of yet, not fully developed.

AUTISM. Using the broadest (and likely oldest) of all definitions, I defined autism as it has been defined within the Merriam-Webster collegiate dictionary (2005) as "a condition or disorder that begins in childhood and causes problems in forming relationships and communicating with other people."

ASPERGER'S SYNDROME. Now considered to be an essentially "defunct diagnoses" (American Psychiatric Association 2013), Asperger's syndrome, as it was originally proposed by Wing (1981), was defined within this proposal as the diagnostic name given to explain the problems of children and adults who exhibited features of autism, but spoke grammatically, and yet, were socially aloof. In her original report, Wing (1981) added that these individuals have been especially difficult to identify, because those who have worked with them often believe that autism is defined by mutism or total social withdrawal. Wing suggested the use of Asperger's syndrome for the condition, to credit the work of Hans Asperger (1944), the first physician to report on individuals exhibiting these conditions. Asperger's syndrome was adopted for clinical use in the third edition of the *Diagnostic and Statistical Manual of Mental Health Disorders* (American Psychiatric Association, 1980) and the term was used until 2014 until it was once again removed from the DSM in June, when the fifth edition of the *Diagnostic and Statistical Manual of Mental Health Disorders* (American Psychiatric Association, 2013) was released. DSM-5 incorporates the core features of Asperger's syndrome into the broader category of autism spectrum disorder (APA, 2013). Although it did not concur with DSM for three years, in 2015 (and with new knowledge that Asperger sent over forty children to death camps in Nazi Germany), the international billing code (ICD-11) finally came into line with DSM-5 to remove the term Asperger's syndrome from the diagnosis. This made the diagnoses of Asperger's syndrome obsolete worldwide. While I avoided this term in my own writing unless it specifically related to official diagnoses, a number of the individuals in the book used it loosely to identify themselves as "higher-functioning."

AUTISM SPECTRUM DISORDER (ASD). ASD is the currently approved DSM-5 term for the full continuum of developmental disorders that manifests with: communication deficits (responding inappropriately in conversations, misreading nonverbal interactions, or having difficulty building age-appropriate friendships); over dependence on routines; high sensitivity to changes in the environment; and intense focus that is often inappropriate (APA, 2013). Within this definition, the symptoms of people with ASD are believed to fall on a continuum, from mild to severe, and these symptoms must be present by early childhood, even if they are not recognized until later according to the APA (2013). The current definition, adopted professionally in June of 2014, is a criteria change from previous definitions adopted to encourage earlier diagnosis of ASD while also recognizing people whose symptoms might not be fully recognized until later, when social demands exceed their capacity to receive the diagnosis (APA, 2013). Both Asperger's syndrome and the previously diagnosed umbrella term "pervasive developmental disorder not otherwise specified" were eliminated in the revision (DSM-5, 2014) to include those individuals with the very "highest functioning" forms of autism. Specifically for those individuals who would not otherwise meet criteria for ASD given normal expressive language development, the diagnoses of "social communication disorder" was also added to DSM-V (APA, 2013). In this book, ASD and autism are used interchangeably to denote both the newest and oldest definitions of the condition.

COGNITION. In its most complete and simplest form, the definition "all of our mental abilities" (Glass & Holyoak, 1986, 2) was adopted as the definition of cognition for this book.

CONSTRUCTIONISM AND CONSTRUCTIVISM. The terms "constructivism" and "constructionism" are often used interchangeably, particularly within discussions about theoretical frameworks throughout the literature. However, for clarity, I chose to follow Crotty's (1998) delineation of these terms which specifies that constructionism can be distinguished from constructivism as the "collective generation and transmission of meaning" (58), instead of just the "meaning-making activity of the individual" (58). Therefore, throughout the research paper that was the basis for the book, the term "constructivism" was applied to both the grounded theory methodology that was used in the study as well as to the meaning-making process for the individual. "Constructionism" was used to depict the shared construction and creation process between myself and my research participants.

GIFTED. While there is not a universally accepted definition of giftedness, according to the National Association for Gifted Children (NAGC):

> Gifted individuals are those who demonstrate outstanding levels of aptitude (defined as an exceptional ability to reason and learn) or competence (documented performance or achievement in top 10 percent or rarer) in one or more domains (NAGC, 2010, 1).

NAGC furthered that the domains in which an individual can demonstrate giftedness include "any structured area of activity with its own symbol system (e.g., mathematics, music, language) and/or set of sensorimotor skills (e.g., painting, dance, sports)" (NAGC, 2010, 1). NAGC added within its definition that:

> Some gifted individuals with exceptional aptitude may not demonstrate outstanding levels of achievement ... due to physical or learning disabilities ... [therefore] identification of these students will need to emphasize aptitude rather than relying only on demonstrated achievement (NAGC, 2010, 1).

This definition was supported by Brown et al. (2005). The current federal definition of the term recognizes that high achievement in areas such as intellectual, creative, artistic, or leadership capacity or in specific academic fields is combined with the need for services or activities not ordinarily provided by the school in order to fully develop those capabilities constituted giftedness (No Child Left Behind Act of 2001). Within this book, the broad federal definition currently in use for the term "giftedness" was applied.

GROUNDED THEORY. Grounded theory is a term most often associated with a specific set of systematic and inductive methods for conducting qualitative research that utilizes strong empirical foundations in the pursuit of answering research questions. As such, the primary goal of grounded theory study is to analyze the data in such a way as to construct new theory that is then able to explain the research phenomena in question (Charmaz, 2009). Within grounded theory methodologies, researchers might utilize flexible research procedures in general, yet when it comes to the collection and analysis of the data, these are handled within explicit, sequential guidelines. More specifically, unlike other forms of qualitative inquiry, grounded theory research follows detailed guidelines to establish how researchers will handle and analyze the data, integrate and streamline their analysis, construct the conceptual findings that will be forwarded as themes, and legitimize the constructed theory toward the advancement of scientific inquiry (Charmaz, 2009). While there is some dispute about the exact methodologies that should be applied when conducting grounded theory research, even when these are considered among its proponents, I chose to adhere to the constructivist methodology of grounded theory research as it was proposed and forwarded by Charmaz (1995, 2006). Using this constructivist branch, the term "grounded theory," as used throughout the research paper behind this book, specifically applies to the grounded theory method as it has been detailed by Charmaz (1995).

INTELLIGENCE. For this work and for the dissertation from which it was built, as it has been formally defined in the historical literature for nearly 100 years, intelligence was defined as the specific and relatively independent group of brain functions that have the ability to predict academic achievement and, thereby, dictate occupational success (Spearman & Spearman, 1973; Ryan, Sautter, Capps, Meneese, & Barth, 1992). Within this definition, the broader definitions of intelligence such as Gardner's (1993) theories on multiple intelligence were not formally considered or discussed in this work.

INTELLIGENCE QUOTIENT (IQ). Using the most recent Wechsler (2003) definition, an individual's IQ is "the composite of (IQ) test scores that assesses cognitive functioning in several specific cognitive domains and provides valid numbers that represent one's overall, general intellectual ability" (2003, 1).

SAVANT. Treffert (1988), one of the primary researchers on the topic of savant syndrome in autism, provided the following definition of the savant with autism: "a juxtaposition of mental handicap and prodigious mental ability" (563). While somewhat controversial, particularly for the assumption that savant skills are derived within high or even prodigious mental abilities, this definition was used for the research and the book.

SENSORY PROCESSING. Sensory processing, as it was used here, was defined as the "neurological process that organizes sensations from one's own body and from the environment making it possible to use the body effectively within the environment" (Ayres, 1972, 11). Within this definition, the assumption that sensory processing acts as the primary interface between the internal workings of the cognitive processing system and the outward demonstration of ability through oral or visual-motor functioning, as described by Minshew, Goldstein, and Siegel (1997) is clearly indicated.

TWICE-EXCEPTIONALITY. According to the NEA (2006), twice exceptional (2e) individuals have both exceptional ability and disability. According to Baldwin, Omdal, and Pereles (2015), this definition of twice-exceptionality suggested that the condition results "in a unique set of circumstances; their exceptional ability may dominate, hiding their disability; their disability may dominate, hiding their exceptional ability; each may mask the other so that neither is recognized or addressed" (2015, 3). In previous definitions, the National Education Association (NEA) also suggested that twice-exceptionality is characterized by asynchronous cognitive development that is accompanied by demonstrated evidence of learning, social, emotional, sensory, or behavioral conditions that significantly interfere with successful school performance (NEA, 2006). Under special education law, IDEA (2004) recognized thirteen disability categories (United States Department of Education, 2004) and within these, ASD is recognized as a disabling condition that can occur in children who are gifted. However, the NEA (2006) also recognized that challenges in identification may occur and cited Baum (1990), adding three categories from which twice-exceptional students may be found. These include: (a) formally identified as gifted, but not having an identified disability—giftedness masks disability; (b) formally identified as having a disability, but not gifted—disability masks giftedness; (c) not formally identified as gifted or disabled—components mask one another—giftedness and the disability not readily apparent. The NEA (2006) recommended that, given the complexity of identifying twice-exceptional learners, a variety of different assessments, formal and informal observations, and reports from those who are familiar with the individual be used to make any identification decisions. These definitions of twice-exceptionality were all taken into account in the use of the term for this book.

REFERENCES

Alloway, T. P., & Alloway, R. G. (2013). Working memory in development. In T. P. Alloway & R. G. Alloway (Eds.), *Working memory: The connected intelligence* (pp. 63-82). New York: Psychology Press.

Amaral, D. G., Schumann, C. M., & Nordahl, C. W. (2008). Neuroanatomy of autism. *Trends in Neurosciences, 31*(3), 137-145. Retrieved from http://fitchlab.com/FitchLab-Bin/NeuroDev%20Downloads/32.Amaral.etal.2008.PDF

Amend, E. R., Schuler, P. A., Beaver-Gavin, K., & Beights, R. (2009). A unique challenge: Sorting out the differences between giftedness and Asperger's disorder. *Gifted Child Today Magazine, 32*(4), 57. Retrieved from http://files.eric.ed.gov/fulltext/EJ860954.pdf

American Psychiatric Association. (1980). *Diagnostic and statistical manual of mental disorders* (3rd ed.). Washington, DC: Author.

American Psychiatric Association. (2013). *Autism spectrum disorder.* Arlington, VA: American Psychiatric Publishing. Retrieved from http://www.dsm5.org/Documents/Autism%20Spectrum%20Disorder%20Fact%20Sheet.pdf

American Psychiatric Association. (2013). *Diagnostic and statistical manual of mental disorders* (5th ed.). Washington, DC: Author.

Arendt, R. E., MacLean, W. E., & Baumeister, A. (1992). Critique of sensory integration therapy and its application in mental retardation. *American Journal of Mental Retardation, 92*(5), 401-416.

Armstrong. T. (2010). *Neurodiversity: Discovering the extraordinary gifts of autism, ADHD, dyslexia, and other brain differences.* Cambridge: Da Capo Press.

Armstrong, T. (2011). *The power of neurodiversity: Unleashing the advantages of your differently wired brain.* Cambridge: Da Capo Press.

Aron, E. N., & Aron, A. (1997). Sensory-processing sensitivity and its relation to introversion and emotionality. *Journal of Personality and Social Psychology, 73*, 345-368. Retrieved from http://www.recoveryonpurpose.com/upload/Sensory%20Processing%20Sensitivity.pdf

Asperger, H. (1944). Die "aunstisehen Psychopathen" im Kindesalter. *Archiv fur psychiatrie und Nervenkrankheiten, 117*, 76-136.

Assouline, S. G., & Whiteman, C. S. (2011). Twice-exceptionality: Implications for school psychologists in the post–IDEA 2004 era. *Journal of Applied School Psychology, 27*(4), 380-402. doi:10.1080/15377903.2011.616576

Ausubel, D. P. (1977). The facilitation of meaningful verbal learning in the classroom. *Educational Psychologist, 12*(2), 162-178. doi:10.1080/00461527709529171

Ayres, J., (1969). Deficits in sensory integration in educationally handicapped children. *Journal of Learning Disabilities, 2*(3), 44–52. doi:10.1177/002221946900200307

Ayres, J. A. (1972). Improving academic scores through sensory integration. *Journal of Learning Disabilities, 5*, 338-343. doi:10.1177/002221947200500605

Ayres, J. (1979). *Sensory integration and the child.* Torrance, CA: Western Psychological Services.

Babiracki, J. L. (2002). *Embracing differences: Adults with high-functioning autism. Listening to the voices of adults with high-functioning autism* (Order No. 3068101). Available from ProQuest Dissertations and Theses Global. (305462956). Retrieved from http://0-search.proquest.com.source.unco.edu/docview/305462956?accountid=12832

Bakley, S. (2001). Through the lens of sensory integration: A different way of analyzing challenging behavior. *Young Children, 56*(6), 70-76. Retrieved from ERIC data base (EJ652626)

Baldwin, L., Omdal, S. N., & Pereles, D. (2015). Beyond stereotypes understanding, recognizing, and working with twice-exceptional learners. *Teaching Exceptional Children, 20*(10), 1-10. doi:10.1177/0040059915569361

Baron-Cohen, S. (1989). The autistic child's theory of mind: A case of specific developmental delay. *Journal of Child Psychology and Psychiatry, 30*(2), 285-297. Retrieved from https://www.researchgate.net/profile/SimonBaron-Cohen/publication/20633551_The_Autistic_Child's_Theory_of_Mind_a_Case_of_Specific_Developmental_Delay/links/0deec5173ac63497d4000000.pdf

Baron-Cohen, S. (1997). *Mindblindness: An essay on autism and theory of mind.* Cambridge, MA: MIT Press.

Baron-Cohen, S., Jolliffe, T., Mortimore, C., & Robertson, M. (1997). Another advanced test of theory of mind: Evidence from very high functioning adults with autism or Asperger syndrome. *Journal of Child Psychology and Psychiatry, 38*(7), 813-822. Retrieved from https://www.researchgate.net/profile/Simon_Baron-Cohen/

publication/13865444_Another_Advanced_Test_of_Theory_of_Mind_Evidence_
from_Very_High_Functioning_Adults_with_Autism_or_Asperger_Syndrome/
links/0deec5173ac6744e9e000000.pdf

Baron-Cohen, S., Leslie, A. M., & Frith, U. (1985). Does the autistic child have a "theory of mind?" *Cognition, 21*(1), 37-46. Retrieved from http://autismtruths.org/pdf/3.%20
Does%20the%20autistic%20child%20have%20a%20theory%20of%20mind_SBC.pdf

Baron-Cohen, S., Ring, H. A., Wheelwright, S., Bullmore, E. T., Brammer, M. J.,
Simmons, A., & Williams, S. C. (1999). Social intelligence in the normal and autistic
brain: An fMRI study. *European Journal of Neuroscience, 11*(6), 1891-1898. Retrieved
from http://docs.autismresearchcentre.com/papers/1999_BCetal_FMRI.pdf

Baron-Cohen, S., Ring, H. A., Bullmore, E. T., Wheelwright, S., Ashwin, C., & Williams, S. C. (2000). The amygdala theory of autism. *Neuroscience and Biobehavioral Reviews, 24*(3), 355-364. Retrieved from http://www.utdallas.edu/~tres/neuroII/trautman.
pdf

Baron-Cohen, S., Wheelwright, S., Burtenshaw, A., & Hobson, E. (2007). Mathemat-
ical talent is linked to autism. *Human Nature, 18*(2), 125-131. doi:10.1007/s12110-007-
9014-0

Baron-Cohen, S., Lombardo, M., Tager-Flusberg, H., & Cohen, D. (Eds.). (2013). *Understanding other minds: Perspectives from developmental social neuroscience.* Oxford: University Press.

Bartak, L. & Rutter, M. (1976). Differences between mentally retarded and normally
intelligent autistic children. *Journal of Autism and Childhood Schizophrenia, 6*, 109-120.
doi:10.1007/BF01538054

Baum, (1990). Gifted but learning disabled: A puzzling paradox. *ERIC Clearinghouse on
Disabilities in Education.* Retrieved from http://www.hoagiesgifted.org/eric/e479.html

Baum, W. M. (2005). *Understanding behaviorism: Behavior, culture, and evolution.* Mal-
den, MA: Blackwell Publishing.

Bauman, M. L., & Kemper, T. L. (2005). Neuroanatomic observations of the brain
in autism: A review and future directions. *International Journal of Developmental Neuroscience, 23*(2), 183-187. Retrieved from https://scholar.google.com/scholar?q=Neu-
roanatomic+observations+of+the+brain+in+autism%3A+a+review+and+future+direc-
tions&btnG=&hl=en&as_sdt=0%2C6

Ben-Sasson, A., Hen, L., Fluss, R., Cermak, S. A., Engel-Yeger, B., & Gal, E. (2009). A meta-analysis of sensory modulation symptoms in individiuals with autism spectrum disorders. *Journal of Autism and Developmental Disorders, 39*, 1-11. Retrieved from https://scholar.google.com/scholar?q=A+meta-analysis+of+sensory+modulation+symptoms+in+individiuals+with+autism+spectrum+disorders&btnG=&hl=en&as_sdt=0%2C6

Bettelheim, B. (1967). *The empty fortress.* New York: Simon and Schuster.

Blaikie, N. (2007). *Approaches to social enquiry: Advancing knowledge.* Cambridge: Polity Press.

Bodner, K. E., Williams, D. L., Engelhardt, C. R., & Minshew, N. J. (2014). A comparison of measures for assessing the level and nature of intelligence in verbal children and adults with autism spectrum disorder. *Research in Autism Spectrum Disorders, 8*(11), 1434-1442. Retrieved from http://dx.doi.org/10.1016/j.rasd.2014.07.015

Boud, D., Keogh, R., & Walker, D. (Eds.). (2013). *Reflection: Turning experience into learning.* London: Routledge.

Boulet, S., Schieve, L., Cohen, R. A., Blumberg, S. J., Yeargin-Allsop, M., & Kogan, M. D. (2011). Trends in the prevalence of developmental disabilities in U.S. children, 1997-2008. *Pediatrics, 127*(6), 1034-1042. Retrieved from http://pediatrics.aappublications.org/content/early/2011/05/19/peds.2010-2989.full.pdf

Bower, G. H. (1970). Imagery as a relational organizer in associative learning. *Journal of Verbal Learning and Verbal Behavior, 9*(5), 529-533. Retrieved from http://ilearn.ssis.asia/pluginfile.php/17383/mod_resource/content/1/Bower%201970.pdf

Bowler, D. M. (1992). "Theory of Mind" in Asperger's Syndrome Dermot M. Bowler. *Journal of Child Psychology and Psychiatry, 33*(5), 877-893. Retrieved from https://www.researchgate.net/profile/Dermot_Bowler/publication/230222692_Theory_of_Mind_in_Asperger's_Syndrome_Dermot_M._Bowler/links/5537c66a0cf247b8587b5839.pdf

Bowler, D. M., Matthews, N. J., & Gardiner, J. M. (1997). Asperger's syndrome and memory: Similarity to autism but not amnesia. *Neuropsychologia, 35*(1), 65-70. Retrieved from http://www.ncbi.nlm.nih.gov/pubmed/8981378

Broderick, A. & Ne'eman, A. (2008). Autism as metaphor: Narrative and counter narrative. *International Journal of Inclusive Education, 12*, 459-476.

Brown, S. W., Renzulli, J. S., Gubbins, E. J., Siegle, D., Zhang, W., & Chen, C. H. (2005). Assumptions underlying the identification of gifted and talented students.

REFERENCES

Gifted Child Quarterly, 49(1), 68-79. Retrieved from http://www.gifted.uconn.edu/ sem/pdf/assumptions_identification.pdf

Bruner, J. S. (1961). The act of discovery. *Harvard Educational Review.* Retrieved from psycabstracts database (36:01:1FD21B)

Bryson, S. E., & Smith, I. M. (1998). Epidemiology of autism: Prevalence, associated characteristics, and implications for research and service delivery. *Mental Retardation and Developmental Disabilities Research Reviews, 4*(2), 97-103. doi:10.1002/(SICI)1098-2779(1998)4:2<97::AID-MRDD6>3.0.CO;2-U

Burger-Veltmeijer, A. E., Minnaert, A. E., & Van Houten-Van den Bosch, E. J. (2011). The co-occurrence of intellectual giftedness and autism spectrum disorders. *Educational Research Review, 6*(1), 67-88. Retrieved fromhttp://eppl604-autism-and-creativity.wm-wikis.net/file/view/sdarticle-20.pdf/198323102/sdarticle-20.pdf

Burr, V. (2003). *Social constructionism.* New York: Routledge.

Buzan, T., & Buzan, B. (1993). *The mind map book.* London: BBC Books.

Cabeza, R., & Kingstone, A. (Eds.). (2006). *Handbook of functional neuroimaging of cognition.* Cambridge: MIT Press.

Cahan, S., & Gejman, A. (1993). Constancy of IQ scores among gifted children. *Roeper Review, 15*(3), 140-143. doi:10.1080/02783199309553488

Carroll, J. B. (1993). *Human cognitive abilities: A survey of factor-analytic studies.* New York: Cambridge University Press.

Carver, L. J., & Dawson, G. (2002). Development and neural bases of face recognition in autism. *Molecular Psychiatry, 7,* S18. Retrieved from https://www.researchgate.net/ profile/Leslie_Carver/publication/11239072_Development_and_neural_bases_of_ face_recognition_in_autism/links/004635339a88ab8a09000000.pdf

Case-Smith, J. (2002). Effectiveness of school-based occupational therapy intervention in handwriting. *The American Journal of Occupational Therapy, 56*(1), 17-25. doi:10.5014/ ajot.56.1.17

Cash, A. B. (1999). A profile of gifted individuals with autism: The twice-exceptional learner. *Roeper Review, 22*(1), 22-27. doi:10.1080/02783199909553993

Centers for Disease Control. (2014, February). CDC estimates 1 in 68 children has been identified with autism spectrum disorder. *Centers for Disease Control Morbidity and*

Mortality Report (64), RR–2. Retrieved from http://www.cdc.gov/media/releases/2014/
p0327-autism-spectrum-disorder.html

Cermak, S. A., & Henderson, A. (1990). The efficacy of sensory integration procedures.
Sensory Integration Quarterly, 18(1), 1-5. Retrieved from http://www.spdfoundation.net/
files/9714/2430/1237/cermak.pdf

Charman, T., Pickles, A., Simonoff, E., Chandler, S., Loucas, T., & Baird, G. (2011).
IQ in children with autism spectrum disorders: Data from the Special Needs and Autism Project (SNAP). *Psychological Medicine, 41*(03), 619-627. Retrieved from http://cen-
taur.reading.ac.uk/17903/1/IQ_(in_press)_Psychological_Medicine.pdf

Charmaz, K. (2003). Grounded theory. In J.A. Smith (Ed), *Qualitative psychology: A
practical guide to research methods* (pp. 81-110). New York: Sage.

Charmaz, K. (2006). *Constructing grounded theory*. London: Sage.

Charmaz, K. (2009). Grounded theory. In L. M. Given (Ed.), *The SAGE encyclopedia of
qualitative research methods* (pp. 374-376). New York: SAGE.

Charmaz, K. (2014). *Constructing grounded theory*. New York: Sage.

Cermak, S., & Henderson, A. (1990). The efficacy of sensory integration procedures.
Sensory Integration Quarterly, 18, 28-36. Retrieved from http://spdfoundation.net/pdf/
cermak.pdf

Cisek, P., & Kalaska, J. F. (2010). Neural mechanisms for interacting with a world full
of action choices. *Annual Review of Neuroscience, 33*, 269-298. Retrieved from http://
www.im-clever.eu/documents/courses/computational-embodied-neuroscience-1/CEN/
files/CisekKalaska2010NeuralMechanismsForInteractingWithAWorldFullOfAction-
Choices.pdf

Cohn, E., Miller, L. J., & Tickle-Degnen, L. (2000). Parental hopes for therapy outcomes: Children with sensory modulation disorder. *The American Journal of Occupational
Therapy, 54*, 36-43. Retrieved from http://sinetwork.publishpath.com/Websites/sinet-
work/files/Content/4385046/cohn_miller.pdf

Collins, A., Greeno, J., Resnick, L. B., Berliner, B., & Calfee, R. (1992). Cognition and
learning. In D. C. Berliner & R. C. Calfee (Eds.), *Handbook of Educational Psychology*
(pp.15-46). New York: Simon & Shuster MacMillan.

Colom, R., Escorial, S., Shih, P. C., & Privado, J. (2007). Fluid intelligence, memory span, and temperament difficulties predict academic performance of young adolescents. *Personality and Individual differences, 42*(8), 1503-1514. Retrieved from http://www.web. teaediciones.com/Ejemplos/Colom_2007_Gf_memory%20span%20and%20temperament%20difficulties.pdf

Corbin, J., & Strauss, A. (2014). *Basics of qualitative research: Techniques and procedures for developing grounded theory.* Sherman Oaks, CA: Sage publications.

Courchesne, E., & Pierce, K. (2005). Why the frontal cortex in autism might be talking only to itself: Local over-connectivity but long-distance disconnection. *Current Opinion in Neurobiology, 15*(2), 225-230. Retrieved from http://sinetwork.publishpath.com/Websites/sinetwork/files/Content/4385046/cohn_miller.pdf

Courchesne, E., Townsend, J., Akshoomoff, N. A., Saitoh, O., Yeung-Courchesne, R., Lincoln, A. J., ... & Lau, L. (1994). Impairment in shifting attention in autistic and cerebellar patients. *Behavioral Neuroscience, 108*(5), 848. Retrieved from http://infantlab.fiu.edu/articles/Courchesne,%20Townsend%20et%20al%201994%20Behav%20Neuroscience.pdf

Crane, L., Goddard, L., & Pring, L. (2009). Sensory processing in adults with autism spectrum disorders. *Autism, 13*(3), 215-228. Retrieved from https://www.researchgate.net/profile/Lorna_Goddard/publication/24280447_Crane_L_Goddard_L_Pring_L_Sensory_processing_in_adults_with_autism_spectrum_disorders_Autism_13_215-228/links/0fcfd513f5d47e8425000000.

Currenti, S. A. (2010). Understanding and determining the etiology of autism. *Cellular and Molecular Neurobiology, 30*(2), 161-171. Retrieved from http://static.springer.com/sgw/documents/1379063/application/pdf/Autism1.pdf

Dabrowski, K. (1966). The theory of positive disintegration. International Journal of *Psychiatry, 2*(2), 229-249. Retrieved from http://positivedisintegration.com/

Dąbrowski, K., Kawczak, A., & Sochanska, J. (1973). *The dynamics of concepts.* London: Cryf.

Daniels, S., & Piechowski, M., (2008). *Living with intensity: Understanding the sensitivity, excitability, and emotional development of gifted children, adolescents, and adults.* Scottsdale, AZ: Great Potential Press.

Dawson, G., Carver, L., Meltzoff, A. N., Panagiotides, H., McPartland, J., & Webb, S. J. (2002). Neural correlates of face and object recognition in young children with autism spectrum disorder, developmental delay, and typical development. *Child Development, 73*(3), 700-717. Retrieved from http://www.ncbi.nlm.nih.gov/pmc/articles/ PMC3651041/

Dawson, M., Soulières, I., Gernsbacher, M. A., & Mottron, L. (2007). The level and nature of autistic intelligence. *Psychological Science, 18*(8), 657-662. Retrieved from http:// www.ncbi.nlm.nih.gov/pmc/articles/PMC4287210/

Deary, I. J., Der, G., & Ford, G., (2001). Reaction times and intelligence differences: A population-based cohort study. *Intelligence, 29*(5), 389-399. doi:10.1016/S0160-2896(01)00062-9

Deci, E. L., Vallerand, R. J., Pelletier, L. G., & Ryan, R. M. (1991). Motivation and education: The self-determination perspective. *Educational Psychologist, 26*(3-4), 325-346. Retrieved from http://sdtheory.s3.amazonaws.com/SDT/documents/1991_DeciValle-randPelletierRyan_EP.pdf

DeMyer, M. K., Barton, S., Alpern, G. D., Kimberlin, C., Allen, J., Yang, E., & Steele, R. (1974). The measured intelligence of autistic children. *Journal of Autism and Childhood Schizophrenia, 4*(1), 42-60. doi:10.1007/BF02104999

Descartes, R., & Cottingham, J. (1985). *Meditationes de prima philosophia* (Vol. 2). Cambridge: University Press.

DiMatties, M. E., & Sammons, J. H. (2003). *Understanding sensory integration.* Retrieved from ERIC Clearinghouse (ED478564)

Domjan, M. (2014). *The principles of learning and behavior.* Stamford, CT: Cengage Learning.

Donnelly, J. A., & Altman, R. (1994). The autistic savant: Recognizing and serving the gifted student with autism. *Roeper Review, 16*, 252-255. doi:10.1080/02783199409553591

Duncan, J. (1986). Disorganisation of behaviour after frontal lobe damage. *Cognitive Neuropsychology, 3*(3), 271-290. doi:10.1080/02643298608253360

Dunn, W. (1997). The impact of sensory processing abilities on the daily lives of young children and their families: A conceptual model. *Infants and Young Children, 9*(4), 23-35. Retrieved from http://img2.timg.co.il/forums/71501742.pdf

Ebbinghaus, H. (1913). *Memory: A contribution to experimental psychology* (No. 3). University Microfilms. Retrieved from https://books.google.com/

books?hl=en&lr=&id=oRSMDF6y3l8C&oi=fnd&pg=PA62&dq=Memo-ry%3B+a+contribution+to+experimental+psychology+by+Ebbinghaus,+Hermann,+1850-1909&ots=RkyTNA6Zhz&sig=tKficFJ-dUWKjxRMotrlp2S024E#v=o-nepage&q=Memory%3B%20a%20contribution%20to%20experimental%20psychology%20by%20Ebbinghaus%2C%20Hermann%2C%201850-1909&f=false

Egly, R., Driver, J., & Rafal, R. D. (1994). Shifting visual attention between objects and locations: Evidence from normal and parietal lesion subjects. *Journal of Experimental Psychology: General, 123*(2), 161. Retrieved from http://www.psych.utoronto.ca/users/ferber/teaching/visualattention/readings/Oct13/1994_Egly_etal_JEPG.pdf

Egon, G. (2005). Paradigmatic controversies, contradictions, and emerging confluences. In N. K. Denzin & Y. S. Lincoln (Eds). *The SAGE handbook of qualitative research* (3rd ed.) (pp. 97-128). Thousand Oaks, CA: SAGE.

Ehlers, S., Nyden, A., Gillberg, C., Dahlgren Sandberg, A., Dahlgren, S-O., Hjelm-quist, E., & Oden, A. (1997). Asperger Syndrome, autism, and attention disorders: A comparative study of cognitive profiles of 120 children. *Journal of Child Psychology and Psychiatry, 38*, 207-217. doi:10.1111/j.1469-7610.1997.tb01855.x

Einfeld, S. L., & Tonge, B. J. (1996). Population prevalence of psychopathology in children and adolescents with intellectual disability: II epidemiological findings. *Journal of Intellectual Disability Research, 40*(2), 99-109. doi:10.1046/j.1365-2788.1996.768768.x

Eldevik, S., Hastings, R. P., Hughes, J. C., Jahr, E., Eikeseth, S., & Cross, S. (2009). Meta-analysis of early intensive behavioral intervention for children with autism. *Journal of Clinical Child and Adolescent Psychology, 38*(3), 439-450. doi: 10.1080/15374410902851739

Every Student Succeeds Act of 2015, Pub. L. No. 114-95 § 114, Stat. 1117 (2015). Retrieved from https://www.congress.gov/bill/114th-congress/senate-bill/1177/text#toc-H5BC3D91709FA473FBD463E0BBD12695D

Facon, B. (2008). How does the strength of the relationships between cognitive abilities evolve over the life span for low-IQ vs high-IQ adults? *Intelligence, 36*(4), 339-349. Retrieved from http://dx.doi.org/10.1016/j.intell.2007.11.004

Fatemi, S. H., Halt, A. R., Realmuto, G., Earle, J., Kist, D. A., Thuras, P., & Merz, A. (2002). Purkinje cell size is reduced in cerebellum of patients with autism. *Cellular and Molecular Neurobiology, 22*(2), 171-175. doi:10.1023/A:1019861721160

Fenton, A., & Krahn, T. (2007). Autism, neurodiversity, and equality beyond the "normal." *Journal of Ethics in Mental Health, 2*(2), p. 2. Retrieved from http://philpapers.org/rec/FENANA

Flynn, J. R. (1987). Massive IQ gains in 14 nations: What IQ tests really measure. *Psychological Bulletin, 101*(2), 171-191. Retrieved from http://www.iapsych.com/iqmr/fe/LinkedDocuments/flynn1987.pdf

Flynn, J. R. (2007). *What is intelligence?: Beyond the Flynn effect.* Cambridge: Cambridge University Press.

Foley-Nicpon, M., Assouline, S., & Stinson, R. D. (2012). Cognitive and academic distinctions between gifted students with autism and Asperger syndrome. *Gifted Child Quarterly, (56)*2, 77-89. doi:10.1177/0016986211433199

Fombonne, E., Bolton, P., Prior, J., Jordan, H., & Rutter, M. (1997). A family study of autism: Cognitive patterns and levels in parents and siblings. *Journal of Child Psychology and Psychiatry, 38*(6), 667-683. doi:10.1111/j.1469-7610.1997.tb01694.x

Frith, U. (1970). Studies in pattern detection in normal and autistic children: I. Immediate recall of auditory sequences. *Journal of abnormal psychology, 76*(3p1), 413. Retrieved from https://www.researchgate.net/profile/Uta_Frith/publication/17688587_Studies_in_pattern_detection_in_normal_and_autistic_children._I._Immediate_recall_of_auditory_sequences._Journal_of_Abnormal_Psychology_76(3)_413-420/links/02e7e51602d-1d5ae49000000.pdf

Frith, U., & Happé, F. (1994). Autism: Beyond "theory of mind." *Cognition, 50*, 115-132. doi:10.1016/0010-0277(94)90024-8. Retrieved from https://wiki.inf.ed.ac.uk/twiki/pub/ECHOES/MindTheory/Frith1994.pdf

Frye, D., Zelazo, P. D., & Palfai, T. (1995). Theory of mind and rule-based reasoning. *Cognitive Development, 10*(4), 483-527. Retrieved from https://www.researchgate.net/profile/Philip_Zelazo2/publication/223863150_Theory_of_Mind_and_rule-based_reasoning/links/55bb137908ae9289a0928217.pdf

Gallagher, J. J., & Reis, S. M. (Eds.). (2004). *Public policy in gifted education* (Vol. 12). Thousand Oaks, CA: Corwin Press.

Gardner, H. (1993). *Multiple intelligences. The theory in practice.* New York: Basic Books.

Gazzaniga, M. S. (Ed.). (2004). *The cognitive neurosciences.* Cambridge, MA: MIT

Gere, D. R., Capps, S. C., Mitchell, D. W., & Grubbs, E. (2009). Sensory sensitivities of gifted children. *American Journal of Occupational Therapy, 63*(3), 288-295. doi: 10.5014/ajot.63.3.288

Ghaziuddin, M. (2010). Brief report: Should the DSM V drop Asperger syndrome? *Journal of Autism and Developmental Disorders, 40*(9), 1146-1148.) doi:10.1111/j.1469-7610.1997.tb01694.x

Gilbert, P. (1996). Asperger's syndrome. In *The AZ Reference Book of Syndromes and Inherited Disorders* (pp. 40-43). New York: Springer.

Gilbert, C. D., & Sigman, M. (2007). Brain states: Top-down influences in sensory processing. *Neuron, 54*(5), 677-696. Retrieved from http://www.sciencedirect.com/science/article/pii/S0896627307003765

Gilman, B. J., Lovecky, D. V., Kearney, K., Peters, D. B., Wasserman, J. D., Silverman, L. K., ... & Rimm, S. B. (2013). Critical issues in the identification of gifted students with co-existing disabilities, the twice-exceptional. *Sage Open, 3*(3), 2158244013505855. doi:10.1177/2158244013505855

Glaser B. G. (1967). *The discovery of grounded theory.* Chicago, IL: Aldine Publishing.

Glaser, B. G. (1978). *Theoretical sensitivity: Advances in the methodology of grounded theory.* Mill Valley, CA: Sociology Press.

Glaser, B. G. (1992). *Emergence vs forcing: Basics of grounded theory analysis.* Mill Valley, CA: Sociology Press.

Glaser, B. S., & Strauss, A. (1968). A.(1967). The discovery of grounded theory. *Strategies for qualitative research.* London: Weidenfeld and Nicolson.

Glass, A. L., & Holyoak, K. J. (1986). *Cognition* (2nd ed.). New York: Random House.

Grandin, T. A. (2010, September). *Journey to the center of my brain.* Paper presented at the meeting of the United States Autism and Asperger Association World Conference, Salt Lake City, UT.

Guba, E. G., & Lincoln, Y. S. (1989). *Fourth generation evaluation.* Newbury Park, CA: Sage. Retrieved from http://www.wmich.edu/evalctr/archive_checklists/constructivisteval.pdf

Guilfoyle, C. (2006). NCLB: Is there life beyond testing? *Educational Leadership, 64*(3), 8. Retrieved from http://scsnl.stanford.edu/documents/Greicius_Default-Mode_Activity_04.pdf

Hala, S., & Russell, J. (2001). Executive control within strategic deception: A window on early cognitive development? *Journal of Experimental Child Psychology, 80*(2), 112-141.

Hansotia, P. (2003). A neurologist looks at mind and brain: "The enchanted loom." *Clinical Medicine and Research, 1*(4), 327-332. doi: http://dx.doi.org/10.1006/jecp.2000.2627

Happé, F., Briskman, J., & Frith, U. (2001). Exploring the cognitive phenotype of autism: Weak "central coherence" in parents and siblings of children with autism: I. Experimental tests. *Journal of Child Psychology and Psychiatry, 42*(3), 299-307. doi:10.1111/1469-7610.00723

Harris, S. L., Handleman, J. S., Gordon, R., Kristoff, B., & Fuentes, F. (1991). Changes in cognitive and language functioning of preschool children with autism. *Journal of autism and developmental disorders, 21*(3), 281-290. doi: 10.1007/BF02207325

Hart, D., Grigal, M., & Weir, C. (2010). Expanding the paradigm: Postsecondary education options for individuals with autism spectrum disorder and intellectual disabilities. *Focus on Autism and Other Developmental Disabilities, 25*(3), 134-150. doi:10.1177/1088357610373759

Hashimoto, T., Tayama, M., Murakawa, K., Yoshimoto, T., Miyazaki, M., Harada, M., & Kuroda, Y. (1995). Development of the brainstem and cerebellum in autistic patients. *Journal of Autism and Developmental Disorders, 25*(1), 1-18. doi:10.1007/BF02178163

Heaton, P., & Wallace, G. L. (2004). Annotation: The savant syndrome. *Journal of Child Psychology and Psychiatry, 45*(5), 899-911. doi:10.1111/j.1469-7610.2004.t01-1-00284.x

Helms, J. E. (1992). Why is there no study of cultural equivalence in standardized cognitive ability testing? *American Psychologist, 47*(9), 1083. Retrieved from http://psycnet.apa.org/doi/10.1037/0003-066X.47.9.1083

Herbert, M. R. (2005). Autism: A brain disorder or a disorder that affects the brain. *Clinical Neuropsychiatry, 2*(6), 354-379. Retrieved from http://learningmethods.net/downloads/pdf/martha.herbert--autism-brain.disorder.or.disorder.affecting.brain.pdf

Hermelin, B. & O'connor, N. (1970). *Psychological experiments with autistic children.* Oxford, England: Pergamon.

Hermelin, B., & O'connor, N. (1971). Spatial coding in normal, autistic and blind children. *Perceptual and motor skills, 33*(1), 127-132. Retrieved from http://www.amsciepub.com/doi/pdf/10.2466/pms.1971.33.1.127

REFERENCES

Hill, E. L., & Bird, C. M. (2006). Executive processes in Asperger syndrome: Patterns of performance in a multiple case series. *Neuropsychologia, 44*(14), 2822-2835. Retrieved from http://research.gold.ac.uk/2561/1/hill&bird_neuropsychologia06_GRO.pdf

Hippler, K., & Klicpera, C. (2003). A retrospective analysis of the clinical case records of "autistic psychopaths" diagnosed by Hans Asperger and his team at the University Children's Hospital, Vienna. *Philosophical Transactions of the Royal Society of London. Series B: Biological Sciences, 358*(1430), 291-301. Retrieved from http://www.ncbi.nlm.nih.gov/pmc/articles/PMC1693115/pdf/12639327.pdf

Holzinger, K., & Swineford, F. (1942). *A study in factor analysis: The reliability of bi-factors and their relation to other measures.* Chicago, IL: The University of Chicago Press.

Howlin, P., & Asgharian, A. (1999). The diagnosis of autism and Asperger syndrome: Findings from a survey of 770 families. *Developmental Medicine and Child Neurology, 41*(12), 834-839. Retrieved from http://onlinelibrary.wiley.com/doi/10.1111/j.1469-8749.1999.tb00550.x/pdf

Huber, D. H. (2007). *Clinical presentation of autism spectrum disorders in intellectually gifted students* (Doctoral dissertation). Retrieved from https://books.google.com/books?hl=en&lr=&id=eby-FW0IUGcC&oi=fnd&pg=PA1&dq=Clinical+presentation+of+autism+spectrum+disorders+in+intellectually+gifted+students+&ots=1r_ZnYg-sE&sig=vyFF6IY3YBGz7X2-QFYUN45Q3X8#v=onepage&q=Clinical%20presentation%20of%20autism%20spectrum%20disorders%20in%20intellectually%20gifted%20students&f=false

Huberman, M., & Miles, M. B. (2002). *The qualitative researcher's companion.* New York: Sage.

Jensen, A. R. (2000). Charles E. Spearman: The discoverer of g. *Portraits of Pioneers in Psychology, 4,* 97-116. Retrieved from http://arthurjensen.net/wp-content/uploads/2014/06/Charles-Spearman-Discoverer-of-g-2000-by-Arthur-Robert-Jensen.pdf

Jeong, Y., Son, J. W., Kim, B. N., & Yoo, H. J. (2015). Evolutionary Perspective on Autism. *Journal of the Korean Academy of Child and Adolescent Psychiatry, 26*(2), 67-74. doi: 10.5765/jkacap.2015.26.2.67

Joseph, R. M., Tager-Flusberg, H., & Lord, C. (2002). Cognitive profiles and social-communicative functioning in children with autism spectrum disorder. *Journal of Child Psychology and Psychiatry, 43*(6), 807-821. Retrieved from http://www.ncbi.nlm.nih.gov/pmc/articles/PMC1201493/

Kanaya, T., Scullin, M. H., & Ceci, S. J. (2003). The Flynn effect and US policies: The impact of rising IQ scores on American society via mental retardation diagnoses. *American Psychologist, 58*(10), 778. Retrieved from http://www.udesarrollo.cl/biblioteca/scl/2005/diciembre/FP_006.pdf

Kanner, L. (1943). Autistic disturbances of affective contact. *Nervous child, 2*(3), 217-250. Retrieved from http://neurodiversity.com/library_kanner_1943.pdf

Kanner, L. (1971). Follow-up study of eleven autistic children originally reported in 1943. *Journal of Autism and Childhood Schizophrenia, 1*(2), 119-145. Retrieved from http://www.neurodiversity.com/library_kanner_1971.pdf

Kaplan, L. (2011). U.S. college autism project. *USAAA Weekly Newsletter.* Retrieved from http://www.usautism.org/uscap/index.htm

Kapp, S. K., Gillespie-Lynch, K., Sherman, L. E., & Hutman, T. (2012, April 30). Deficit, difference, or both? Autism and neurodiversity. *Developmental Psychology.* Advance Online Publication. doi:10.1037/a0028353

Kasari, C., & Lawton, K. (2010). New directions in behavioral treatment of autism spectrum disorders. *Current Opinion in Neurology, 23*(2), 137. Retrieved from http://www.ncbi.nlm.nih.gov/pmc/articles/PMC4324974/

Kendall, P. C., & Hollon, S. D. (Eds.). (2013). *Cognitive-behavioral interventions: Theory, research, and procedures.* New York: Academic Press.

Kint, M. G. (1977). Problems for families vs. problem families. *Schizophrenia Bulletin, 3*(3), 355-356. doi: 10.1093/schbul/3.3.355

Klin, A. (2000). Attributing social meaning to ambiguous visual stimuli in higher-functioning autism and Asperger syndrome: the Social Attribution Task. *Journal of Child psychology and Psychiatry, 41*(7), 831-846. Retrieved from https://www.researchgate.net/profile/Ami_Klin/publication/12249162_Attributing_Social_Meaning_to_Ambiguous_Visual_Stimuli_in_Higherfunctioning_Autism_and_Asperger_Syndrome_The_Social_Attribution_Task/links/5486fb600cf268d28f06f977.pdf

Kranowitz, C. S. (1998). *The out of sync child: Recognizing and coping with sensory processing disorder.* New York: Berkeley Publishing.

Larson, S. A., Lakin, K. C., Anderson, L., Lee, N. K., Lee, J. H., & Anderson, D. (2001). Prevalence of mental retardation and developmental disabilities: Estimates from the 1994/1995 National Health Interview Survey Disability Supplements.

Journal Information, 106(3). Retrieved from http://www.aaiddjournals.org/doi/abs/10.1352/0895-8017%282001%29106%3C0231%3APOMRAD%3E2.0.CO%3B2?-journalCode=ajmr.1

Leekam, S. R., Nieto, C., Libby, S. J., Wing, L., & Gould, J. (2007). Describing the sensory abnormalities of children and adults with autism. *Journal of autism and developmental disorders, 37*(5), 894-910. Retrieved from http://psych.cf.ac.uk/home2/leekam/2007%20JADD%20Leekam%20sensory.pdf

Little, C. A., Feng, A. X., VanTassel-Baska, J., Rogers, K. B., & Avery, L. D. (2007). A study of curriculum effectiveness in social studies. *Gifted Child Quarterly, 51*(3), 272-284. doi: 10.1177/0016986207302722

Lincoln, A. J., Courchesne, E., Kilman, B. A., Elmasian, R., & Allen, M. (1988). A study of intellectual abilities in high-functioning people with autism. *Journal of Autism and Developmental Disorders, 18*(4), 505-524. doi:10.1177/0016986207302722

Lord, C., Rutter, M., Goode, S., Heemsbergen, J., Jordan, H., Mawhood, L., & Schopler, E. (1989). Autism diagnostic observation schedule: A standardized observation of communicative and social behavior. *Journal of autism and developmental disorders, 19*(2), 185-212. doi:10.1007/BF02211841

Lovaas, O. I., Schaeffer, B., & Simmons, J. Q. (1965). Building social behavior in autistic children by use of electric shock. *Journal of Experimental Research in Personality, 1*(2), 99-109. Retrieved from http://psycnet.apa.org/psycinfo/1966-03230-001

Lovaas, O. I., Koegel, R., Simmons, J. Q., & Long, J. S. (1973). Some generalization and follow-up measures on autistic children in behavior therapy. *Journal of Applied Behavior Analysis, 6*(1), 131-165. Retrieved from http://www.ncbi.nlm.nih.gov/pmc/articles/PMC1310815/pdf/jaba00063-0133.pdf

Lovecky, D. V. (2003). *Different minds: Gifted children with AD/HD, Asperger Syndrome, and other learning deficits.* Philadelphia, PA: Jessica Kingsley Publishers

Madsen, K. M., Hviid, A., Vestergaard, M., Schendel, D., Wohlfahrt, J., ... & Melbye, M. (2002). A population-based study of measles, mumps, and rubella vaccination and autism. *New England Journal of Medicine, 347*(19), 1477-1482. doi:10.1056/NEJMoa021134

Manjiviona, J., & Prior, M. (1999). Neuropsychological profiles of children with Asperger syndrome and autism. *Autism, 3*(4), 327-356. doi:10.1177/1362361399003004003

Mann, T. A., & Walker, P. (2003). Autism and a deficit in broadening the spread of visual attention. *Journal of Child Psychology and Psychiatry,44*(2), 274-284. Retrieved from https://wiki.inf.ed.ac.uk/twiki/pub/ECHOES/VisualAttention/Mann2003.

Marco, E. J., Hinkley, L. B., Hill, S. S., & Nagarajan, S. S. (2011). Sensory processing in autism: A review of neurophysiologic findings. *Pediatric Research, 69,* 48R-54R. Retrieved from http://www.nature.com/pr/journal/v69/n5-2/full/pr9201193a.html

Markram, H., Rinaldi, T., & Markram, K. (2007). The intense world syndrome–An alternative hypothesis for autism. *Frontiers in Neuroscience, 1*(1), 77. Retrieved from http://www.ncbi.nlm.nih.gov/pmc/articles/PMC2518049/

Markram, K., & Markram, H. (2010). The intense world theory–a unifying theory of the neurobiology of autism. *Frontiers in human neuroscience, 4,* 224. Retrieved from https://scholar.google.com/scholar?q=Markram+and+Markram%2C+2010&btnG=&hl=en&as_sdt=0%2C6

Mayes, S. D., & Calhoun, S. L. (2003). Ability profiles in children with autism influence of age and IQ. *Autism, 7*(1), 65-80. Retrieved from http://www.corwin.com/upmdata/3913_AUT_V7N1.pdf#page=52

McMahon, W. M., & Ritvo, A. (1989). The UCLA-University of Utah epidemiologic survey of autism prevalence. *American Journal of Psychiatry, 146*(2), 194-199. Retrieved from http://citeseerx.ist.psu.edu/viewdoc/download?doi=10.1.1.456.4606&rep=rep1&type=pdf

Mendaglio, S. (1995). Sensitivity among gifted persons: A multi-faceted perspective. *Roeper Review, 17*(3), 169-172. doi:10.1080/02783199509553652

Mercer, C. D., Jordan, L., Allsopp, D. H., & Mercer, A. R. (1996). Learning disabilities definitions and criteria used by state education departments. *Learning Disability Quarterly, 19*(4), 217-232. doi:10.2307/1511208

Merriam, S. B., & Tisdell, E. J. (2015). *Qualitative research: A guide to design and implementation.* Hoboken, NJ: John Wiley & Sons.

Merriam-Webster's collegiate dictionary (11th ed.). (2005). Springfield, MA: Merriam-Webster.

Miller, J. N., & Ozonoff, S. (1997). Did Asperger's cases have Asperger disorder? A research note. *Journal of Child Psychology and Psychiatry, 38*(2), 247-251. doi:10.1111/j.1469-7610.1997.tb02354.x

Miller, J. N., & Ozonoff, S. (2000). The external validity of Asperger disorder: Lack of evidence from the domain of neuropsychology. *Journal of Abnormal Psychology, 109*(2), 227-239. doi:10.1037/0021-843X.109.2.227

Miller, L. J., Coll, J. R., & Schoen, S. A. (2007). A randomized controlled pilot study of the effectiveness of occupational therapy for children with sensory modulation disorder. *American Journal of Occupational Therapy,61*(2), 228-238. Retrieved from http://citeseerx.ist.psu.edu/viewdoc/download?doi=10.1.1.551.4453&rep=rep1&type=pdf

Miller, L. J., & Lane, S. J. (2000, March). Toward a consensus in terminology in sensory integration theory and practice: Part 1: Taxonomy of neurophysiological processes. Sensory Integration *Special Interest Section Quarterly, 23*, 1–4. Retrieved from http://www.spdfoundation.net/files/1214/2430/1338/TowardaConcensus-Part1.pdf

Miller, L. J., Robinson, J., & Moulton, D. (2004). Sensory modulation dysfunction: Identification in early childhood. *Handbook of infant, toddler, and preschool mental health assessment*. New York: Oxford University Press.

Miller, L. K. (1998). Defining the savant syndrome. *Journal of Developmental and Physical Disabilities, 10*(1), 73-85. doi:10.1023/A:1022813601762

Miller, L. K. (1999). The savant syndrome: Intellectual impairment and exceptional skill. *Psychological Bulletin, 125*(1), 31. doi:10.1037/0033-2909.125.1.31

Minshew, N. J., Goldstein, G., & Siegel, D. J. (1997). Neuropsychologic functioning in autism: Profile of a complex information processing disorder. *Journal of the International Neuropsychological Society, 3*(04), 303-316. Retrieved from http://www.researchgate.net/profile/Daniel_Mcintosh/publication/8504430_Prevalence_of_parents'_perceptions_of_sensory_processing_disorders_among_kindergarten_children/links/54087bd60cf-2c48563bd8284.pdf

Moonlial, J. (2007). *Information processing, psychosocial adjustment, and sensory processing in gifted youth* (Doctoral dissertation, Azusa Pacific University). Retrieved from http://www spdfoundation.net/pdf/sensoryissues

National Association for Gifted Children. (2010). *Redefining giftedness for a new century: Shifting the Paradigm*. Retrieved from http://www.nagc.org/sites/default/files/Position%20Statement/Redefining%20Giftedness%20for%20a%20New%20Century.pdf

National Education Association, (2006). *The twice exceptional dilemma*. Retrieved from http://www.nea.org/assets/docs/twiceexceptional.pdf

National Vaccine Information Center. (2015). *Introduction to autism*. Retrieved from http://www.nvic.org/Vaccines-and-Diseases/Autism.aspx

Nershberg, G. (2010, November 15). I sense, therefore I think [Web log post]. Retrieved from http://cognitivephilosophy.net/consciousness/i-sense-therefore-i-think/

Nichols, M. J., & Newsome, W. T. (1999). The neurobiology of cognition. *Nature, 402*, C35-C38. Retrieved from http://www.neurosci.info/courses/systems/VisualSub/nichols_newsome_1999_cognition.pdf

Nicpon, M. F., Allmon, A., Sieck, B., & Stinson, R. D. (2011). Empirical investigation of twice-exceptionality: Where have we been and where are we going? *Gifted Child Quarterly, 55*(1), 3-17. Retrieved from http://maxwellgate.pbworks.com/w/file/fetch/49309573/GATEResearchDocEmpiricalInvestigationTwice-Exceptionality.pdf

Nicpon, M. F., Doobay, A. F., & Assouline, S. G. (2010). Parent, teacher, and self-perceptions of psychosocial functioning in intellectually gifted children and adolescents with autism spectrum disorder. *Journal of Autism and Developmental Disorders, 40*(8), 1028-1038. doi:10.1007/s10803-010-0952-8

No Child Left Behind Act of 2001, Pub. L. No. 107-110, § 115, Stat. 1425 (2002). Retrieved from http://www.nagc.org/resources-publications/resources/definitions-giftedness#sthash.fEOsFnYZ.dpuf

Norman, D. A., & Shallice, T. (1986). Attention to action. In D. Norman & T. Shallice (Eds.), *Consciousness and self-regulation* (pp.1-18). New York: Springer.

O'Connor, N., & Hermelin, B. (1984). Idiot savant calendrical calculators: Math or memory. *Psychological Medicine, 14*(4), 801-806. doi:10.1017/S0033291700019772

O'Connor, N., & Hermelin, B. (1987). Visual and graphic abilities of the idiot savant artist. *Psychological Medicine, 17*(01), 79-90. doi:10.1017/S0033291700013003

O'Connor, N., & Hermelin, B. (1989). The memory structure of autistic idiot-savant mnemonists. *British Journal of Psychology, 80*(1), 97-111. doi:10.1111/j.2044-8295.1989.tb02305.x

O'Connor, N., & Hermelin, B. (1994). Two autistic savant readers. *Journal of Autism and Developmental Disorders, 24*(4), 501-515. doi:10.1007/BF02172131

O'Reilly, R. & Munakata, Y. (2000). *Computational explorations in cognitive neuroscience: Understanding the mind by simulating the brain*. Cambridge, MA: MIT Press.

REFERENCES

Otsuka, H., Harada, M., Mori, K., Hisaoka, S., & Nishitani, H. (1999). Brain metabolites in the hippocampus-amygdala region and cerebellum in autism: An 1H-MR spectroscopy study. *Neuroradiology, 41*(7), 517-519. doi:10.1007/s002340050795

Ozonoff, S. (1995). Executive functions in autism. In E. Schopler & G. B. Mesibov (Eds.), *Learning and cognition in autism* (pp. 199-219). New York: Springer.

Ozonoff, S., Pennington, B. F., & Rogers, S. J. (1991). Executive function deficits in high-functioning autistic individuals: Relationship to theory of mind. *Journal of Child Psychology Psychiatry, 32*, 1081-1105. doi:10.1111/j.1469-7610.1991.tb00351.x

Ozonoff, S., South, M., & Miller, J. N. (2000). DSM-IV-defined Asperger syndrome: Cognitive, behavioral and early history differentiation from high-functioning autism. *Autism, 4*(1), 29-46. doi:10.1177/1362361300041003

Ozonoff, S., & Strayer, D. L. (1997). Inhibitory function in nonretarded children with autism. *Journal of autism and developmental disorders, 27*(1), 59-77. doi: 10.1023/A:1025821222046

Paivio, A. (1976). *On exploring visual knowledge.* London: University of Western Ontario, Department of Psychology.

Paivio, A. (1991). Dual coding theory: Retrospect and current status. *Canadian Journal of Psychology/Revue Canadienne de Psychologie, 45*(3), 255. Retrieved from http://www.rit.edu/cos/smerc/journalpapers/Paivio_Dual_coding_theory_review.pdf

Pellicano, E., Maybery, M., Durkin, K., & Maley, A. (2006). Multiple cognitive capabilities/deficits in children with an autism spectrum disorder: "Weak" central coherence and its relationship to theory of mind and executive control. *Development and Psychopathology, 18*(01), 77-98. doi:10.1017/S0954579406060056

Piechowski, M., Miller, N., & Daniels, S. (1995). Assessing developmental potential in gifted children: A comparison of methods. *Roeper Review, 17*, 176-181. doi:10.1080/02783199509553654

Pinker, S. (1979). Formal models of language learning. *Cognition, 7*(3), 217-283. Retrieved from http://w.mindstalk.net/indiana/Orals/pinkermodels.pdf

Piven, J., Arndt, S., Bailey, J., & Andreasen, N. (1996). Regional brain enlargement in autism: A magnetic resonance imaging study. *Journal of the American Academy of Child and Adolescent Psychiatry, 35*(4), 530-536. Retrieved from http://dx.doi.org/10.1097/00004583-199604000-00020

Polatajko, H. J., Kaplan, B. J., & Wilson, B. N. (1992). Sensory integration treatment for children with learning disabilities: Its status 20 years later. *OTJR: Occupation, Participation and Health, 12*(6), 323-341. doi: 10.1177/153944929201200601

Posthuma, D., De Geus, E. J., Baaré, W. F., Pol, H. E. H., Kahn, R. S., & Boomsma, D. I. (2002). The association between brain volume and intelligence is of genetic origin. *Nature neuroscience, 5*(2), 83-84. Retrieved from http://dare.ubvu.vu.nl/bitstream/handle/1871/18295/Posthuma_Nature%20Neuroscience_5(2)_2002_u.pdf?sequence=2

Preckel, F., Holling, H., & Vock, M. (2006). Academic underachievement: Relationship with cognitive motivation, achievement motivation, and conscientiousness. *Psychology in the Schools, 43*(3), 401-411. doi:10.1002/pits.20154

Premack, D., & Woodruff, G. (1978). Does the chimpanzee have a theory of mind? *Behavioral and Brain Sciences, 1*(04), 515-526. Retrieved from http://is.muni.cz/el/1423/podzim2012/PSY277/um/36127513/PREMACK_WOODRUFF_cimpanzees.pdf

Prince-Hughes, D. (Ed.). (2002). *Aquamarine blue 5: Personal stories of college students with autism.* Ohio: University Press.

Prior, M. R. (1979). Cognitive abilities and disabilities in infantile autism: A review. *Journal of Abnormal Child Psychology, 7*(4), 357-380. doi: 10.1007/BF00917609

Provost, B., Lopez, B. R., & Heimerl, S. (2007). A comparison of motor delays in young children: Autism spectrum disorder, developmental delay, and developmental concerns. *Journal of Autism and Developmental Disorders, 37*(2), 321-328. Retrieved from https://www.cdd.unm.edu/ecspd/pubs/pdfs/comparisonofmotordelays.pdf

Rajendran, G., & Mitchell, P. (2007). Cognitive theories of autism. *Developmental Review, 27*(2), 224-260. Retrieved from http://strathprints.strath.ac.uk/5154/1/strathprints008124.pdf

Rao, V. S., & Ashok, M. V. (2013). Intelligence in autism. *Indian Journal of Psychological Medicine, 35*(4), 428. doi:10.4103/0253-7176.122254

Redcay, E., & Courchesne, E. (2005). When is the brain enlarged in autism? A meta-analysis of all brain size reports. *Biological Psychiatry, 58*(1), 1-9. Retrieved from http://dx.doi.org/10.1016/j.biopsych.2005.03.026

Risi, S., Lord, C., Gotham, K., Corsello, C., Chrysler, C., Szatmari, P., ... & Pickles, A. (2006). Combining information from multiple sources in the diagnosis of autism spectrum disorders. *Journal of the American Academy of Child and Adolescent Psychiatry, 45*(9),

1094-1103. Retrieved from http://dx.doi.org/10.1097/01.chi.0000227880.42780.0e

Robertson, J. M. (Ed.). (2013). *The philosophical works of Francis Bacon*. New York: Routledge.

Rogers, S. J., & Ozonoff, S. (2005). Annotation: What do we know about sensory dysfunction in autism? A critical review of the empirical evidence. *Journal of Child Psychology and Psychiatry, 46*(12), 1255-1268. doi:10.1111/j.1469-7610.2005.01431.x

Ryan, T. V., Sautter, S. W., Capps, C. F., Meneese, W., & Barth, J. T. (1992). Utilizing neuropsychological measures to predict vocational outcome in a head trauma population. *Brain Injury, 6*(2), 175-182. doi:10.3109/02699059209029656

Sarter, M., Givens, B., & Bruno, J. P. (2001). The cognitive neuroscience of sustained attention: Where top-down meets bottom-up. *Brain Research Reviews, 35*(2), 146-160. Retrieved from http://faculty.psy.ohio-state.edu/bruno/PDF%20files/top%20down%20ms.pdf

Sattler, J. M. (1988). *Assessment of children*. San Diego, CA: JM Sattler.

Sattler, J. M. (2008). *Assessment of children: Cognitive foundations*. La Mesa, CA: JM Sattler.

Schalock, R. L., Luckasson, R. A., & Shogren, K. A. (2007). The renaming of mental retardation: Understanding the change to the term intellectual disability. *Journal Information, 45*(2), 116-124. Retrieved from http://dev.deathpenaltyinfo.org/documents/renamingMRIDDApril2007.pdf

Scheuffgen, K., Happé, F., Anderson, M., & Frith, U. (2000). High "intelligence," low "IQ"? Speed of processing and measured IQ in children with autism. *Development and psychopathology, 12*(1), 83-90. Retrieved from https://scholar.google.com/scholar?q=High%22+intelligence%2C%22+low%22+IQ%22%3F+Speed+of+processing+and+measured+IQ+in+children+with+autism&btnG=&hl=en&as_sdt=0%2C6

Schopler, E., Andrews, C. E., & Strupp, K. (1979). Do autistic children come from upper-middle-class parents? *Journal of Autism and Developmental Disorders, 9*(2), 139-152. doi:10.1007/BF01531530

Sergeant, J. A., Geurts, H., & Oosterlaan, J. (2002). How specific is a deficit of executive functioning for attention-deficit/hyperactivity disorder? *Behavioural Brain Research, 130*(1), 3-28. doi:10.1016/S0166-4328(01)00430-2

Shettleworth, S. J. (1999). *Cognition, evolution, and behavior.* Oxford, UK: Oxford University Press.

Shmulsky, S., & Gobbo, K. (2013). Autism spectrum in the college classroom: Strategies for instructors. *Community College Journal of Research and Practice, 37*(6), 490-495. doi: 10.1080/10668926.2012.716753

Shomstein, S., & Yantis, S. (2002). Object-based attention: Sensory modulation or priority setting?. *Perception & psychophysics, 64*(1), 41-51. Retrieved from https://www.researchgate.net/profile/Steven_Yantis/publication/11448919_Objectbased_attention_sensory_modulation_or_priority_setting/links/00463518b926edb779000000.pdf

Silberman, S. (2015). *NeuroTribes: The legacy of autism and the future of neurodiversity.* New York: Penguin Random House.

Silverman, L. K. (1997). The construct of asynchronous development. *Peabody Journal of Education, 72*(3-4), 36-58. Retrieved from http://positivedisintegration.com/Silverman1997.pdf

Skinner, B. F. (1953). *Science and human behavior.* New York: The Free Press, Simon and Schuster.

Solms, M., & Turnbull, O. (2002). *The brain and the inner world: An introduction to the neuroscience of subjective experience.* London, UK: Karnac Books.

Spearman, C. (1904). "General Intelligence," objectively determined and measured. *The American Journal of Psychology, 15*(2), 201-292. Retrieved from http://www.jstor.org/stable/1412107?seq=1#page_scan_tab_contents

Spearman, C. E., & Spearman, C. (1973). *The nature of "intelligence" and the principles of cognition.* New York: Arno Press.

Stent, G. S. (1975). Limits to the scientific understanding of man. *Science, 187*(4181), 1052-1057. doi:10.1126/science.1114334

Sternberg, R. J., Grigorenko, E. & Bundy, D. A. (2001). The predictive value of IQ. *Merrill-Palmer Quarterly, 47*(1), 1-41. doi:10.1353/mpq.2001.0005

Sternberg, R. J., & Wagner, R. K. (1993). The g-ocentric view of intelligence and job performance is wrong. *Current Directions in Psychological Science, (2)*1, 1-5. Retrieved from Shettleworth, S. J. (1999). Cognition, evolution, and behavior. Oxford, UK: Oxford University Press.

REFERENCES

Strauss, A. L. (1987). *Qualitative analysis for social scientists.* Cambridge University Press.

Stroop, J. R. (1935). Studies of interference in serial verbal reactions. *Journal of Experimental Psychology, 18*(6), 643. Retrieved from http://psychcentral.com/classics/Stroop/

Swedo, S. E., Baird, G., Cook, E. H., Happé, F. G., Harris, J. C., Kaufmann, W. E., ... & Wright, H. H. (2012). Commentary from the DSM-5 workgroup on neurodevelopmental disorders. *Journal of the American Academy of Child and Adolescent Psychiatry, 51*(4), 347-349.

Szatmari, P., Bryson, S. E., Boyle, M. H., Streiner, D. L., & Duku, E. (2003). Predictors of outcome among high functioning children with autism and Asperger syndrome. *Journal of Child Psychology and Psychiatry, 44*(4), 520-528. doi:10.1111/1469-7610.00141

Tabachnick, B. G., & Fidell, L. S. (2013). *Using multivariate statistics* (6th ed.). Upper Saddle River, NJ: Pearson Education Inc.

Terman, L. M. (1931). *The gifted child.* Stanford, California: Stanford University.

Tinbergen, E. A., & Tinbergen, N. (1972). *Early childhood autism: An ethological approach.* Berlin: Parey.

Treffert, D. A. (1988). The idiot savant: A review of the syndrome. *American Journal of Psychiatry, 145*(5), 563-572. Retrieved from http://0-search.proquest.com.source.unco.edu/docview/220469203?accountid=12832

Treffert, D. A. (1999). The savant syndrome and autistic disorder. *CNS Spectrums, 4*(12), 57. doi:10.1017/S1092852900006830

Treffert, D. A. (2005). The savant syndrome in autistic disorder. In M. F. Casanova (ed.). *Recent developments in autism research* (pp. 27-55). New York, NY: Nova Science Publishers.

Treffert, D. A. (2009). The savant syndrome: An extraordinary condition. A synopsis: Past, present, future. *Philosophical Transactions of the Royal Society B: Biological Sciences, 364*(1522), 1351-1357. Retrieved from http://rstb.royalsocietypublishing.org/content/364/1522/1351.short

Treffinger, D. J., & Renzulli, J. S. (1986). Giftedness as potential for creative productivity: Transcending IQ scores. *Roeper Review, 8*(3), 150-154. doi:10.1080/02783198609552960

Trikalinos, T. A., Karvouni, A., Zintzaras, E., Ylisaukko-Oja, T., Peltonen, L., Järvelä, I., & Ioannidis, J. P. A. (2006). A heterogeneity-based genome search meta-analysis for autism-spectrum disorders. *Molecular Psychiatry, 11*(1), 29-36. Retrieved from http://www.nature.com/mp/journal/v11/n1/full/4001750a.html

Trochim, W., & Donnelly, J. (2001). Research Methods Knowledge Base. Ithaca, New York: Cornell University.

Tuchman, R., & Rapin, I. (2002). Epilepsy in autism. *The Lancet Neurology, 1*(6), 352-358. doi:10.1080/02783198609552960

Tucker-Drob, E. M. (2009). Differentiation of cognitive abilities across the lifespan. *Developmental Psychology, 45*(4), 1097. Retrieved from http://www.ncbi.nlm.nih.gov/pmc/articles/PMC2855504/

United States Autism and Asperger Association, (2014). Who we are. Retrieved from http://www.usautism.org/about_us.htm

United States Department of Education, (2004). Building the legacy: IDEA 2004. Retrieved from http://idea.ed.gov/explore/view/p/,root,regs,300,A,300%252E8,c,

Van Krevelen, D. A. (1971). Early infantile autism and autistic psychopathy. *Journal of Autism and Childhood Schizophrenia, 1*, 82-86. Retrieved from http://www.neurodiversity.com/library_van_krevelen_1971.pdf

Vargas, S., & Camilli, G. (1999). A meta-analysis of research on sensory integration treatment. *American Journal of Occupational Therapy, 53*(2), 189-198. Retrieved from http://fileserver.daemen.edu/~rholmstr/si_meta_analysis1999.pdf

von Glasersfeld, E. (1989). Cognition, construction of knowledge, and teaching. *Synthese, 80*(1), 121-140. ERIC database [381352]

Voss, J. F. (1978). Cognition and instruction: Toward a cognitive theory of learning. In R. H. Bruning, G. J. Schraw, & M. N. Norby (Eds.), *Cognitive psychology and instruction* (pp. 13-26). New York: Springer.

Vygotsky, L. S. (1962). *Language and thought*. Ontario, Canada: Massachusetts Institute of Technology Press.

Watson, J. B. (1925). *Behaviorism*. Livingston, NJ: Transaction Publishers.

Wechsler, D. (2003). *Wechsler intelligence scale for children—4th ed.* (WISC-IV). San Antonio, TX: The Psychological Corporation.

Weimer, A. K., Schatz, A. M., Lincoln, A., Ballantyne, A. O., & Trauner, D. A. (2001).

REFERENCES

"Motor" impairment in Asperger syndrome: Evidence for a deficit in proprioception. *Journal of Developmental and Behavioral Pediatrics, 22*(2), 92-101.). Retrieved from http://journals.lww.com/jrnldbp/Abstract/2001/04000/_Motor__Impairment_in_Asperger_Syndrome__Evidence.2.aspx

Wellman, H. M., Cross, D., & Watson, J. (2001). Meta-analysis of theory-of-mind development: the truth about false belief. *Child development, 72*(3), 655-684. Retrieved from http://www.academicroom.com/article/meta-analysis-theory-mind-development-truth-about-false-belief

Werner, G. (2007). Perspectives on the neuroscience of cognition and consciousness. *BioSystems, 87*(1), 82-95. Retrieved from http://cogprints.org/4809/1/perspectivemanu.pdf

Wicherts, J. M., Dolan, C. V., Hessen, D. J., Oosterveld, P., Van Baal, G. C. M., Boomsma, D. I., & Span, M. M. (2004). Are intelligence tests measurement invariant over time? Investigating the nature of the Flynn effect. *Intelligence, 32*(5), 509-537. doi: https://www.gwern.net/docs/2004-wicherts.pdf

Wilson, B. A., Alderman, N., Burgess, P. W., Emslie, H., & Evans, J. J. (2003). Behavioural assessment of the dysexecutive syndrome. In P. Rabbitt (Ed.), *Methodology of frontal and executive functioning* (pp. 232-239). UK: Psychology Press.

Wimmer, H., & Perner, J. (1983). Beliefs about beliefs: Representation and constraining function of wrong beliefs in young children's understanding of deception. *Cognition, 13*(1), 103-128. Retrieved from http://www.nips.ac.jp/fmritms/conference/references/Mano/Wimmer1983HCognition.pdf

Wing, L. (1981). Asperger's syndrome: A clinical account. *Psychological Medicine: A Journal of Research in Psychiatry and the Allied Sciences, 11*(1), 115-129. doi:10.1017/S0033291700053332

Wittrock, M. C. (1974). Learning as a generative process. *Educational Psychologist, 11*(2), 87-95. doi:10.1080/00461527409529129

Zelazo, P. D., & Frye, D. (1997). Cognitive complexity and control: A theory of the development of deliberate reasoning and intentional action. In M. I. Staminov (ed.). *Language structure, discourse, and the access to consciousness* (pp. 113-153). Amsterdam, The Netherlands: John Behnamins Publishing.

Zimmer, M., Desch, L., Rosen, L. D., Bailey, M. L., Becker, D., Culbert, T. P., ... &

AUTISM IS THE FUTURE

Wiley, S. E. (2012). Sensory integration therapies for children with developmental and behavioral disorders. *Pediatrics, 129*(6), 1186-1189. doi:10.1542/peds.2012-087

Marlo Payne Thurman, PhD

Marlo began work with children diagnosed with ASD in 1986. With group home management and intensive ABA therapy in her early career, she developed a special interest in meeting the unique needs of those individuals who were asynchronously developed into the realms of the "ASD savant." Through her private practice, Ms. Thurman followed her passion and began specializing in assessment, advocacy, cognitive training, sensory and behavior support, and socio-emotional coaching. In 1999 Marlo founded the Brideun Learning Communities and built the Brideun School for Exceptional Children, a play-based, therapeutic school exclusively serving children grades one through eight who were identified as "twice-exceptional." A quarter of the students served in Marlo's school were on the autism spectrum. After closing the school, Marlo founded 2E Consulting Services to provide training and support to individuals and programs working with twice exceptional students and learners with autism. With advanced degrees in both school psychology and special education, Marlo holds board positions with 2E Newsletter and the US Autism and Asperger's Association. She regularly speaks at conferences and trains teachers and mental health practitioners, where several of her talks have resulted in keynote presentations. In addition to her public speaking and private practice work, Ms. Thurman is an adjunct faculty member at the University of Northern Colorado where she teaches preservice educators and in the graduate school's Autism Certification program. Marlo has been recognized for her work by People magazine, The Special Educator, ADDitude Magazine, The New York Times, and National Public Radio as well as numerous local venues. Most recently, Marlo completed a landmark study proposing an alternative sensory-cognitive difference theory based on her extensive discussions and interactions with diagnosed adults. This research was the foundation for this book. Marlo lives in Johnstown, Colorado. In addition to several "quirky" close friends and family members, Ms. Thurman credits her two adult children for teaching her about the value and beauty of being "different-minded."